MW01627588

THE SCIENCE BEHIND SUCCESS

What every leader needs to know about mindset, influence, culture & performance

---

Jayson Krause

Foreword by Steve Mesler

Copyright © 2020 Jayson Krause.

All rights reserved. No part of this book may be reproduced in any form or by any electronic or mechanical means, including information storage and retrieval systems, without permission in writing from the author, except by a reviewer, who is welcome to quote at brief in a review.

Bulk purchase discounts and customized copies are available by contacting the author at https://www.level52.ca/

978-1-7774219-0-8

This book was published with the support of Happful.com

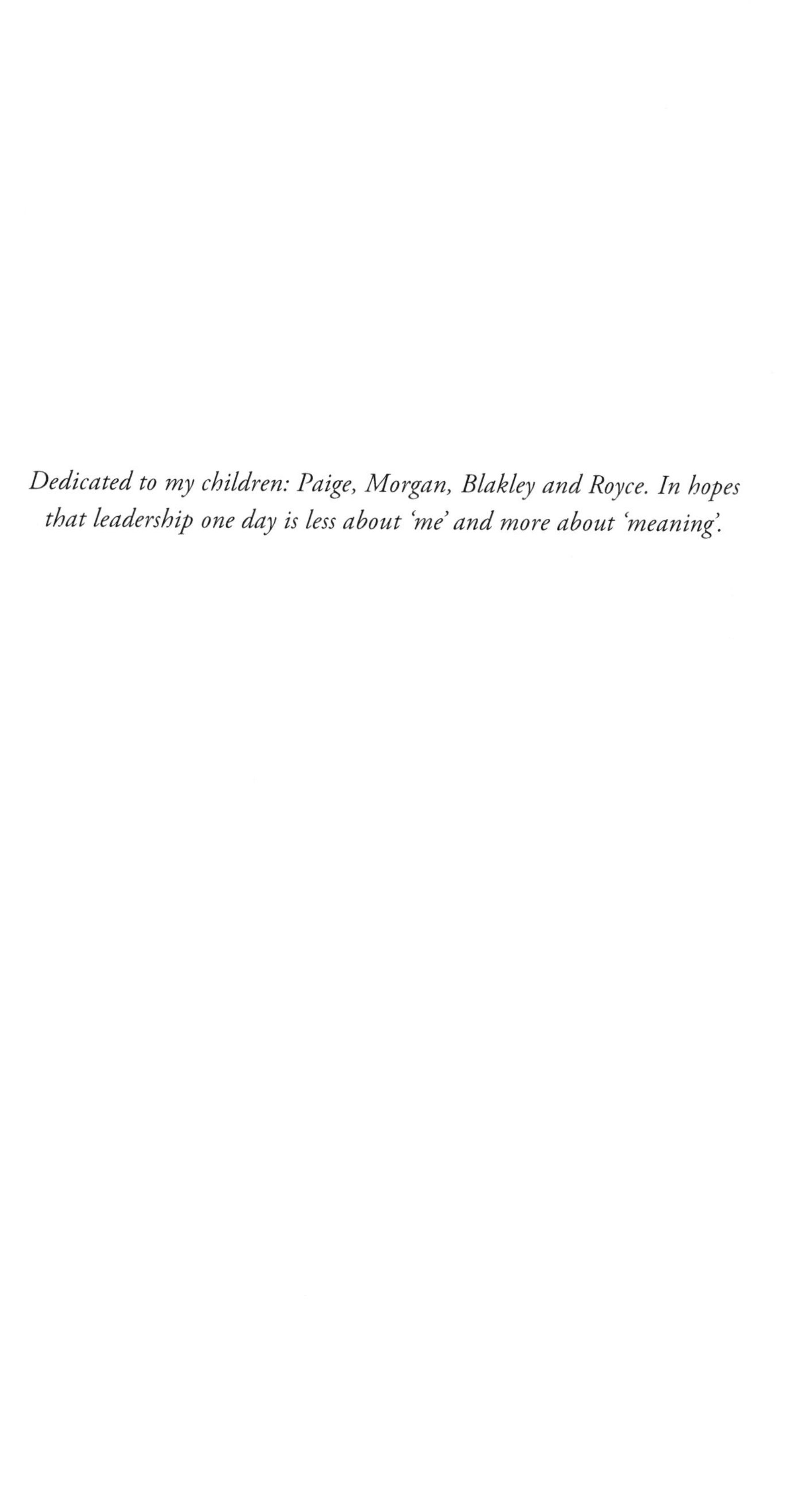

Dedicated to my children: Paige, Morgan, Blakley and Royce. In hopes that leadership one day is less about 'me' and more about 'meaning'.

CONTENTS

FOREWORD

The first time I realized the impact of good, or in this case bad work culture was the moment that changed the trajectory of my life and shaped my thesis on what it means to be a leader to this day.

It was the end of the four-man Olympic bobsled race at the 2006 Winter Olympic Games in Turino, Italy, and I was watching the mighty Germans, led by the greatest bobsledder of all time, Andre Lange, receive their Olympic gold medals. I was supposed to be on that podium. But instead, I was behind a chain link fence, alone, with tears welling up in my eyes as I looked down on what could have been after a seventh place finish. My team was a dysfunctional mess, and this was the worst finish we'd had in four years.

That was the day I drew a line in the sand. I realized that to do anything great in this world I would need to take responsibility for the environment, the relationships, and the culture of the people around me. For in a team sport —which, make no mistake about it, 99% of business is a team sport—the day-to-day is easy to survive with dysfunction, but when the screws tighten you better hope there are no cracks that will cause a rupture. I hadn't ensured that with our 2006 Olympic team, and the consequences were dire.

I made the decision that day to make myself accountable to ensure that I and those around me were set up for success. In the years that followed, I dove deeper into the intricacies of human performance and leadership than I ever knew was possible.

Without fail, by my side through all of it over the past 17 years was Jayson (Jay) Krause—the author of *The Science Behind Success*. We've spent countless hours (probably more like months of time) discussing leadership and strategy over grueling training sessions, coffee conversations and, later on, on the phone during commutes to the office and sitting in diverse boardroom discussions.

Jayson helped me put into perspective the dynamics at play within our four-man bobsled team and how I needed to better understand the unique personalities brought together to perform at sports' highest level. Even as we were competing against each other on the bobsled hill (Jay was a world-class bobsled pilot in his day for Canada), we would check and balance each other's thinking—I was brute force forward and Jay was finesse around the blind corners.

Four years later, almost to the day of that bottoming experience in Italy at the 2006 Olympics, the tables were reversed. I was still looking down, but this time it was from the top of the 2010 Olympic podium in Whistler, British Columbia, with 20 ounces of circular gold and rock being draped around my neck. I was still looking down at Andre Lange, but this time it was to watch him receive a silver medal. Held together by shared principles and values, our team ended a 62-year drought for our country, and I retired from sport to look for the next great adventure. One of my first calls that night was to Jay and his wife, who were back home expecting their first child.

Within a year of conquering the world of bobsled from separate countries, Jayson and I were united again. This time we were on the same team as we began to put together the concepts of the Science Behind Success™ while management consulting in and around Calgary, Alberta.

Over the last decade, Jayson has been a best friend, a mentor, and a business coach to me. From founding and growing Classroom Champions into a world-renowned education non-profit reaching millions of children around the world and partnering with the likes of NBC, multiple National Olympic Committees, NFL and NHL teams to change the social and emotional (see business soft-skills) development of young students in underserved communities; to sitting on the Board of Directors of the United States Olympic and Paralympic Committee during its most tumultuous time in decades—Jayson has taught me that being a leader is a task best left for those willing to put in the work to lead.

To this day, Jayson's company, Level 52, coaches leaders at my organization, and every leader of people takes Level 52 workshops and courses across Classroom Champions. And they do it pro bono.

Through Jayson's guidance, I've found that whether you're leading a small team down a bobsled track, a staff of 20 working remotely (Classroom Champions), or an organization of thousands (The U.S. Olympic Movement) working with billion dollar budgets, understanding the field of play with your people holds the keys to the kingdom.

Leading teams and growing organizations must be systematic to a large degree and fluid to a smaller degree. Sometimes those "systems" are founded in chaos and forged in struggle, but we all have the ability to choose which ideas and principles we're going to build that structure around.

Jayson's Science Behind Success™ method provides an innovative design for people like Jayson and I—people who were tired of taking complex ideas and dumbing them down. We respected that people want to know the facts and the science, and then just need guidance in applying that to their specific scenario. To us, the basis of performance is science and methodology, mixed with consistent and deliberate practice. And that's what this book brings. Jayson doesn't simply boil down the science into meaningless analogies. He explains the science, the origins of the methodology, and then provides tangible ways to implement on a daily basis.

Jayson Krause's *The Science Behind Success* provides the fundamental building blocks to scaffold what *your* successful company or leadership journey should look like. Jayson takes you on a journey that ends with understanding how to build a winning organizational culture, how to make changes when they're needed, and how to look inside yourself and find the tools you can use to succeed.

You're going to be pushed, but that's what bobsledders do—we push things. Then we get in and go 95 mph with no seatbelts. Let's go!

Steve Mesler

Three-time Olympian, Olympic gold medalist, world champion
Co-founder & CEO, Classroom Champions
Member, Board of Directors, U.S. Olympic and Paralympic Committee

INTRODUCTION

I remember walking into the stadium at the 2006 Winter Olympics opening ceremonies. The hype was *nothing* compared to experiencing the real thing. I wore pride in my eyes, my smile, and the way I strode into the sea of people cheering on their respective countries.

I spotted my parents proudly waving our country's flag among the vast crowd, soaking in the moment. They would no doubt recount, years from now, those subtle moments I would forget in the enormity of the event. I could tell by their glowing faces how proud they were of me.

It's a memory that I can recall quickly and vividly—something I'd envisioned several times. It was the most incredible moment of my life…only, it never happened.

I had visualized this moment so many times inside my head, however, instead of marching proudly into my first Olympics, I was at home watching teammates and fellow athletes living MY story as they paraded into Italy's Torino Olympic stadium in 2006. After eight years of pain and effort, sweat, and grinding away, I felt like I had been cheated by life. As life's moments go, this was near rock bottom.

For most of my twenties, I was clear as clear can be. I woke up every morning with a goal and a purpose. I knew what I had to do and when to do it. I had quadrennial goals, yearly, monthly, weekly, and daily goals that could be measured. My tight group of friends were more like a family—a balance of athletes and childhood friends that formed a tight community of laughter, support, and infantile debauchery. Not only that, but I had also differentiated myself. I soaked up and relished the social benefits of being a national team bobsled driver. Not many people can answer the question, "what do you do?" by saying, "I compete against the world's best by racing bobsleds down mountains at hyper speeds in some of the planet's most beautiful winter locations."

Yet all of that vanished. There I was, completely broken for the first time in my life. I was lost, angry, and carrying the grief and the burden of being a complete failure. I obsessed endlessly over all of the things that led to this personal disaster.

Going into the 2006 Olympic year, I was in the best physical shape of my career. Strong, powerful, and confident—I had several top-10 finishes the previous year—the last thing I was worried about was 'making the Olympics.' I was focused more on what I had to do to fight for a medal.

But oh, how life changes when we least expect it.

My childhood best friend had been fighting non-Hodgkin's lymphoma for several years. He'd oscillate between remission and relapse, and in September of 2005, just a few weeks before the season started, I got a phone call from his wife—she didn't think he was going to make it.

I immediately flew home from training in Montreal and got to be with him while he transitioned out of this world. Although it was hard, it was special. It was a paradoxical moment of peace and beauty mashed up with the internal trembling of fear and what the world might be like without him. He was a high-intensity presence who could never be replaced. The grief was so heavy that deep down inside, I didn't care about being fast or winning races anymore. When you stop caring, you stop performing. Despite my best efforts, I couldn't and didn't meet the standards to represent my country. And just like that, my Olympic pursuit was over.

This moment was the domino that slowly fell into the next and quickly turned my eight-year dream of competing in the Olympics into a personal nightmare. The Olympics came and went without me in it. I slowly limped into the sunset of my athletic career, drowning in shame. For the first time in my life, I didn't know what was down the track. I had no goals, no strategies to navigate the pressure that lay in front of me and no crew to launch me into the next corner or pull brakes when needed. Who was I without the title of 'Olympian'?

This nightmare invited me to examine the value I provided in my world. To shed the story of who I *was* so I could step into exploring the person I really wanted to be. I had labeled myself as a failure, but what was I going to do about it? Wallow in self-pity, or pick myself up and start exploring what was next? In truth, I was tired of falling victim to the seductive trap of external validation. I started the difficult process of liberating myself from this trap, shedding my old biases, and examining the old lies and the barriers I had created for myself. I focused on building a new vision and strategy to do something meaningful.

The years after I retired became an experiment. I took my experience from high performance sport and combined it with my passion to help others, turning my attention to management consulting and leadership strategies. Things really started to fall into place when I teamed up with one of my best friends, 2010 Olympic gold medalist, Steve Mesler. As high performance junkies and avid readers, we understood the physiology, strategies, and environment that create high performance.

One night, we started spit-balling about the principles we were exposed to every day as athletes. We had lived and breathed high performance every day, and it seemed obvious to apply the same principles outside of sport. Then why were businesses not employing similar approaches to lead and operate their organizations? Even if they were, they were often missing the same obsession that athletes bring to their craft.

Steve and I believed we could create something that would break rules and activate better awareness and more inspired action in the business context. Using our experience and knowledge of emerging sports science, we developed an approach to leadership that would engage the disengaged, wake up the sleeping subject matter expert, and slap them in the face (metaphorically of course) to be a better leader.

In 2010, we piloted the first version of what I now call the Science Behind Success™ with MBA students at the Warrington School of Business at the University of Florida. As I look back, it was an embarrassing version of our work, but even then, it had a big impact. It woke students up, and they left seeing their world differently. And when you see your world differently, you can start to engage with it differently.

Steve and I parted ways soon after that when he admitted that management consulting wasn't his path and he moved on to something that was more meaningful to him—founding a charity called Classroom Champions with his sister. But our model was out of the gates, and I was committed to refining it to transform the world, one leader at a time. The pain of my Olympic 'failure' had become less acute—a distant memory. I was on a new trajectory, and I'm still going. Now, you are on it with me.

In this book, I share the tried and tested principles that comprise the Science Behind Success™ model that we use at Level 52 today. Over the years, I have applied these principles to many different levels of leadership, from front-line leaders fighting in the trenches to executives responsible for decisions with billion-dollar consequences. I've had over a decade of willing lab rats—leaders at all levels in both blue chip multinationals and small businesses, in locations from Singapore to Silicon Valley and everywhere in between. Using simple underpinnings of science and high performance athletics principles, I helped these leaders to develop the mindset, tools, and playbook necessary to create new and better results in their organizations. Measurable results—increased engagement, higher customer retention, business growth, millions saved on costs—and more importantly, results that can't be measured: the hundreds of millions of dollars saved when leaders avoid mistakes by focusing on the right things that most people miss.

Here's my request. Make this the book you came here to read. If you want to blast through it and then add it to your trophy case, that's your call. If you want to engage with it and meditate over it like a Zen Kōan, do it. This book is structured to take you through a learning progression as if you were in one of my extended leadership programs. While I won't be there to coach you in real time, each chapter concludes with a summary of key points and four important questions. To get the most of the time you devote to this book, I suggest you take those opportunities to highlight what you want to remember, underscore what feels important to you, and identify ways to exercise the principles so you can transform them into actions for yourself. Whichever way you read this book, make it meaningful for you, so you can create meaning for the people you work with.

One last thing. Be warned, this book is direct. Some of what you read may be considered abrasive or unfiltered. At Level 52, we do not do you the disservice of sugarcoating our process or beating around the bush. I highlight and point out the things other people won't, because you need to hear it. Your results are serious. Your results matter. Now let's get to it.

1

WHAT THE HELL IS LEADERSHIP AND WHAT'S WRONG WITH IT?

Early in my consulting career, I was supporting an organization's internal leadership training when one of the participants emailed me with a really good question:

"Jayson, one thing that I struggle to understand is that if everyone is so great, like they were in the training session, if all these leaders embrace this experience and have a desire for continuous improvement, reflection, and personal growth, then why does it so regularly fail? Why is it that when I was talking to my mentee last week, he told me that his leader NEVER had a one-on-one discussion with him, ever!? It's discouraging to see the company invest in developing us and yet the leaders above us don't do any of it."

Unfortunately, this is the norm in way too many organizations. Every year, companies spend more than $350 billion globally on employee training and development.[1] Despite all of this spending, close to 75% of organizations feel they have poor leadership pipelines, a concerning lack of engagement, and are battling not only to attract top talent, but to keep the talent they have. Somewhere along the line, something keeps going wrong. Instead of developing leaders who are agile, responsive, and trusted, organizations continue to cultivate a leadership culture of entrenched habits and tools. Spend more money, keep doing the same things, and expect different results. The definition of insanity.

Why does leadership still underdeliver? There are more than a few reasons behind this. In my years as a consultant, business leader, and the team leader in high performance sport, I've had a front-row seat to the dark side of leadership. Three common denominators have enjoyed center stage position time and time again: expertise, assholes and their egos, and the powerful vortex.

WHY LEADERS FAIL

EXPERTISE

Wow, Jennifer is awesome at her job. She not only hits her performance goals but shatters them every quarter. What should we do to keep her? We could get creative and find a way to keep her in her area of genius, or we could do the normal thing and just promote her into a leadership position. She delivers results, so she'll be a great leader. Right?

Hold on, does Jennifer even like people?

Doesn't matter, she just has to lead them...

Right now, across the world, thousands of people are being promoted because they are good at solving problems. Somehow, somewhere in the past, someone decided that it made sense to take people out of their area of genius—removing them from what they are amazing at—and make

1 Beer, Finnström, and Schrader. (2016). *Harvard Business Review*. 'Why leadership training fails and what to do about it.' [Online]. Available: https://hbr.org/2016/10/why-leadership-training-fails-and-what-to-do-about-it.

them responsible for developing other people. And just like that, this became the accepted way people are made into leaders.

I use the term 'expert' to describe anyone who has been in their position or industry for several years, usually over a decade. They know it inside-out, they deliver top quality effort and produce top quality results. These people have the hyper focus to deliver and how do you recognize them and keep them inside the ecosystem of your company? Well, you promote them into management.

The problem is, often times when you promote experts into leadership positions, they remain experts with a small side of leadership instead of what they should be, which is leaders with a small side of expertise. They don't know what the hell to do, so they do what they know, and that's be an expert, point out what's wrong, tell people what's right, and become irritated when people can't keep pace with the race that's inside their head.

Much of my work at Level 52 involves working with senior leaders or executives who still have incredibly ingrained habits based on their expertise. They have to do a lot of work to learn and deploy something different. They have to unlearn their expertise so they can be better leaders. This is really hard and really important, and not everyone can or is willing to do it.

Michael Jordan doesn't coach basketball. Wayne Gretzky didn't succeed as a hockey coach, and Jerry Rice never coached professional football. All of them are experts, arguably the best at their craft. Why aren't they coaching?

There's a big difference between strapping on the pads and delivering great results yourself and creating the conditions for meaningful results to happen. We can all agree that expertise has its benefits. There are professions where you definitely want an expert delivering the task. You don't want to get brain surgery from anyone that is not a neurosurgeon. You want a good lawyer dealing with litigation. These are obvious examples.

There are benefits to engaging with expertise, but when it comes to leading others, there are significant downsides.

When you lead through your expertise and people come to you with problems, you likely default to solving their problems for them. Your expertise has a strong gravitational pull that exercises and satiates not only your ego but also your internal reward system. It validates you. The problem is, when you look at the long-term benefit to your organization, you're not serving the greater purpose of your leadership, your people, and the company.

When people come to you with questions and you simply provide them answers, the benefits are minimal and short-sighted. The downsides, however, can be significant to everyone involved. When you train your team to come to you with every problem they have, they'll soon be lining up outside your office and will steal all your time. You'll wonder why you don't have time to do other things as you keep solving every little problem they come to you with. As a result, the individuals on your team won't develop because you haven't challenged them to think, and they won't have the chance to become resourceful change-makers. Instead, you'll be saddled with well-trained automatons limited by the programming you've provided. The organization will also lose out because there is no succession plan beyond you. You will have created a nice little logjam of knowledge and decision-making. All because of your precious expertise.

Another significant downside to expertise relates to cognitive tunneling. Cognitive tunneling happens when you've seen something multiple times before. You become hyper focused on the variables you are used to seeing, and you can make correct and quick decisions. You can understand and process information quickly to come to a resolution. The benefits of cognitive tunneling and the precision that comes with it is a huge asset as a high performing individual. As a leader, however, it can leave you with inattentional blindness to variables that appear outside your beautiful tunnel and you can get stuck on appraising things based on your decade high throne, pointing this way and that way as problems arrive at your intersection like a proud traffic cop rife with authority. Expertise is great. It's important. But it's also a dark and nasty thing that will prevent you from being a meaningful leader.

Experts that transition well into leadership understand that *it is exactly their expertise that will hold them back from leading effectively*. They activate the ability to explore before they appraise. So, if you're open to it, take a good, hard look at your expertise and wave goodbye, because you won't see it for a while. Put it into a safety deposit box and lock it up for a while. Don't worry, you know where it is if you really need it, I just don't want you to have immediate access to it because you'll likely let it creep back in. Once you've put it away, turn around and walk away. This hero's journey will give you far more valuable tools to transform the workplace than your expertise will. That is, if your ego doesn't get in the way.

ASSHOLES AND THEIR EGOS

Terrible leadership can be found by following the pungent stench of excessive ego. Egotistical types of leaders win for themselves. Everyone else is there to serve them and be pawns in their endless game of high performance chess. They blame everyone around them for what's not working and see themselves as the keepers of all things great and glorious. These people often act like they have the answers to everything, yet they are completely unaware of their negative impact. They possess a world-class level of ignorance. Now, having a bit of an ego isn't bad. We all have it, and at times it can serve a purpose. But people who lead with extensive ego do much more damage than good for the business, and more often than not, they can't see it. They literally make the people around them less resourceful. Your ignorance and ego can have a significant and measurable negative impact on others.

Richard Boyatzis illustrated this concept through his research using functional magnetic resonance imaging (fMRI) brain scans.[2] Boyatzis conducted studies where he asked individuals in non-management positions

2 Boyatzis, R. and McKee, A. (2005). *Resonant Leadership: Renewing Yourself*

to reflect on specific examples when leaders created dissonant experiences (experiences triggering negative emotions) and resonant experiences (experiences triggering positive emotions). The results were significant. Fourteen regions of the brain responded when participants were asked about resonant leaders in comparison to only six active regions when asked about dissonant leaders. More importantly, 11 regions of the brain were completely deactivated when thinking about dissonant leaders. Long story short, leaders who are narcissistic and ego driven end up creating less resourceful people. Those people who are the essential resources in your company and hold so much potential will be rendered useless because of the asshole that ignorantly seeks to be the smartest hog in the herd.

The ego loves feeling smart and in power. The more someone climbs the ladder in the organization, the more power and authority they tend to collect. And when someone gets more power and authority, people around them try to please them more and more. They get more attention and more affirmation, and the bubble of their ego expands. Former British Foreign Secretary and neurologist David Owen and Duke University Professor John Davidson calls this the 'hubris syndrome'[3], which is defined as a "disorder of the possession of power, particularly power which has been associated with overwhelming success, held for a period of years."[4]

While certainly undesirable to anyone who has to deal with it, the hubris syndrome is nothing compared to being labeled a 'successful business psychopath.' In 2010, a study was published in the *Journal of Research and Personality* titled 'The Search of the Successful Psychopath.'[5] The study explored the difference between psychopaths who become criminals and

---

and Connecting With Others Through Mindfulness, Hope, and Compassion. Boston: Harvard Business School Press.

3 Owen, D. 2008. 'Hubris syndrome.' *Clin Med* (8):428-32.

4 Hougaard, R. and Carter, J. (2018). 'Ego is the enemy of good leadership.' *Harvard Business Review.* [Online] Available: https://hbr.org/2018/11/ego-is-the-enemy-of-good-leadership.

5 Mullins-Sweatt, S., Glover, N., Derefinko, K., Miller, J., & Widiger, T.

those who become 'successful' business people. The results revealed that both demonstrate the same qualities: they are arrogant, callous, and dishonest. They also experience little remorse for their own poor behaviors, minimize self-blame, exploit people, and are shallow. The best part is, leaders like this don't see themselves as these things. They are, of course, ignorant of their own impact.

If you don't think you are the problem, you are definitely the problem. At Level 52, we steer every leader we work with to examine *how* they are the cause, or at least how they are contributing to all of the problems in their team and organization. It's almost always due to either actions you have or haven't taken. I'm serious about that. A mentor of mine used to tell me that the trail of crumbs always takes you back to the most senior leader.

If you are reading this and feel yourself getting defensive, take a breath. Maybe try looking at a fish tank for a few minutes. If the first thing you notice is your own reflection in the glass, close this book and use it as a paper weight because most of the concepts that you'll read after this chapter will likely be stuff that 'other people' should do. Training and development are for other people, right?

THE POWERFUL VORTEX

CFO asks CEO: "What happens if we invest in developing our people and then they leave us?"

CEO: "What happens if we don't, and they stay?"

Providing people training is one thing. Giving people training *and* the tools and the structures to battle the vortex of forgetting is another thing.

Most leadership development and training programs fall into the trap of providing high energy, entertaining, and inspirational events that are measured by how people feel at the end of each session. The training

(2010). 'The search for the successful psychopath.' *Journal of Research in Personality*, 44(4):554-558. [Online] Available: DOI: 10.1016/j.jrp.2010.05.010.

evokes fleeting moments of insight and excitement followed by the inevitable—getting swallowed back into the powerful vortex of meetings, emails, and business as usual. Most of what you learn in the session is forgotten and lost. I'm not just ranting here, the science tells us that most of it really is forgotten.

Over 100 years ago, Hermann Ebbinghaus studied the reality of learning and memory and found that you are likely to forget more than half of the content you are exposed to in about 20 minutes. If you're lucky, you'll retain, at best, about 20% of the content by using specific tools and approaches. We quickly forget anything we learn if we don't use key structures, or even attempt to retain it. Numerous studies confirm Ebbinghaus's findings: You forget 50% of anything new you've just learned within 20 minutes and on average, will have forgotten over 70% within 24 hours. The visual below illustrates this curve and shows how you'll pretty much forget everything within a week if you don't make an effort to retain the information.

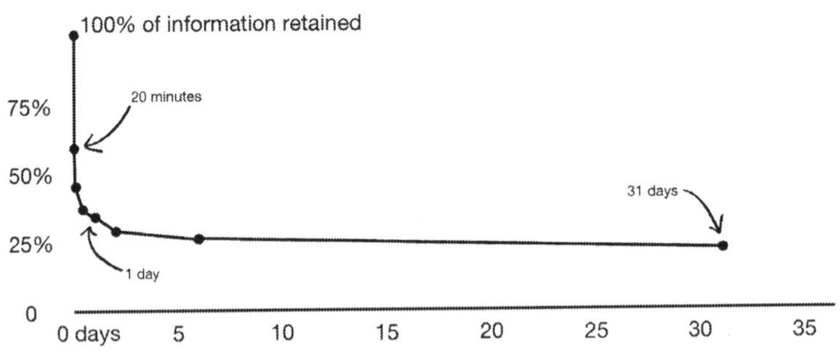

For example, let's say you go to a training seminar on 'Five steps to financial freedom.' You really enjoy the content. The program is well designed, the steps of the process are clear, and there is a detailed, proven approach within each step.

You get more and more excited as the trainer helps you see, feel, and almost taste financial freedom. You have a gorgeous binder rife with rich content summaries and materials that you plan to check back on frequently as you meticulously track your self-driven wealth strategy.

All of this seems so simple and inspiring. Then you leave at the end of the day and go home. That night, you share some of the insights with your significant other, already pausing to try and remember some of the key details to justify why the two of you should use the five-step method.

You go to bed and dream about financial freedom until you get shaken awake by your four-year-old who's just peed the bed. You stumble out of bed and tear off the sheets. After a while, you get everything cleaned up and finally fall back asleep, or at least half asleep, for the remainder of the night. It feels like your brain stem gets torn out when your alarm goes off in the morning, so you reach over and press snooze.

When you finally muster up the energy to get out of bed, you get stuck in an endless game of catch-up. You trick yourself into believing that the harder you try, the more time you'll make up. The day goes by with you jumping from meeting to meeting and phone call to phone call. You stay a little bit later to get that last thing done and finally get home for dinner. The next weekend, while visiting friends, this course comes up in your conversation and you mention a couple of steps in vague detail. You intend to share the resource with your friends, but it never happens. Financial freedom slips away, and all of those neurons that fired during that one-day training session decide to pack their shit and move to a different region of the brain to support the conversation of your latest Netflix binge.

Confused yet? I was too when I first learned about these concepts and the incredible retention, or lack thereof, we're capable of as adults. I've thrown a lot of studies at you already. You are most likely introduced to new concepts or opportunities every day, but you can't and won't do anything to change your circumstances if you rely on your magical gift of natural retention.

The vortex is real and very strong. Watch it and observe every movement. For if you keep this enemy close, you can engage in specific tactics to reduce its gravitational pull and give more force to the changes you need to make to become a meaningful leader. Just remember, if you allow yourself to be unintentional and blindly lumber back into organizational homeostasis, you will hear the flushing sound of your learning potential and time and money investment disappearing into the sewers of lost leadership effectiveness.

Throughout this book, I will underscore the important point that whatever happens after a learning experience is more important than the learning experience itself. In Chapter 6, I'll show you specific strategies that will enable you to flatten the forgetting curve and increase your likelihood to not only remember what you learn, but apply it to deliver meaningful results.

WHAT'S THE VALUE OF A LEADER?

Your expertise, ego, and the powerful vortex combine and contribute to the degradation of your company culture, results, and the value you deliver. But can leadership really influence things that much?

A client once told me, "You will never be out of work because you help organizations with the thing they struggle with the most. The only problem is, most people just don't understand the value of a good leader until they leave."

If you haven't yet found a reason to strengthen your own leadership or the leadership in your organization, consider this. A huge shift has occurred in the last decade in how companies are valued. Recent research conducted by Aon and the Ponemon institute[6] looks at how organizations' tangible and intangible value has changed over time. Tangible assets are things like cash, inventory, equipment, and property—things you can see, feel, and

---

6 Ponemon Institute LLC. '2019 Intangible Assets Financial Statement Impact Comparison Report'. [Online] Available: https://www.aon.com/getmedia/60fbb49a-c7a5-4027-ba98-0553b29dc89f/Ponemon-Report-V24.aspx.

touch. Intangible assets are the opposite. They don't exist in the physical form and are considered 'potential revenue'—things like brand equity, intellectual property, and networks. From 1975 to 2018, intangible assets went from contributing 17% of a company's value on the S&P 500 to an average of 84%, while companies like Amazon and Microsoft's value is figured to be over 90% intangibles. A significant transformation has occurred, shifting the value from physical assets to people-driven ones like intellectual property, brand equity, and relationships. The companies that will thrive moving forward are the ones who know how to inspire, engage, and unlock creativity to unleash even greater intangible value. This is where your leadership comes in.

WHAT THE HELL IS LEADERSHIP?

If expertise, egomania, and the pursuit of maximizing intangible value aren't fertile grounds for disrupting and transforming leadership, then what is?

Let's back up for a minute and explore the definition of leadership. I've found that most leaders don't pause and take the time to *really* explore and understand leadership. And anywhere there isn't clarity, there is debris and confusion that creates drag and leads to unnecessary leakage of energy and resources. I have used the term 'leader' several times in this book already, but what the hell does leadership mean anyhow?

To answer that, I'll tell you a story about Gary.

Gary was a senior employee and mid-level leader inside a global organization Level 52 was delivering an Accelerated Leader Program (ALP) for. Depending on the level of intensity, our ALPs are usually made up of around 15 to 30 leaders over a 12-week process during which we push them, stretch them, and coach them like crazy to become meaningful leaders. During one of our sessions in the midpoint of the program, the discussion became spirited when someone brought up the topic of responsibility and accountability.

Gary was a straight shooter and a bit of a skeptic, of most things. He was a classic expert who knew a lot about a lot of things. At one point in our discussion, he asked in frustration, "Stop for a minute. Can you guys please tell us what the difference between responsibility and accountability is?"

My answer was: "No."

He looked at me with confusion as he probably wondered what they were paying me and my team for.

This is how I responded: "It's less important for me to tell you what the difference between the two is and more important for you to define it for yourself and create meaning, then communicate it clearly, and get alignment with the people you work with. It's what leaders do."

It doesn't serve you to seek one single definition of the 'truth' from someone or somewhere else. The reality is that there are usually multiple shades of truth and understanding depending on the situation and the people you interact with. In our programs, I ask people to take a stab at defining leadership. As you might expect, I get several different definitions of what a leader is, and in a large group of people we rarely, if ever, get multiple people with the same definition. All the definitions of what a leader is or isn't do not really matter. They don't matter because they are just words, and more importantly, someone else's words. Someone else's definition of leadership is trivial and shouldn't matter to you, just like an organization's values and mission statement don't mean anything unless you make them meaningful.

Challenging Gary this way forced him to pause and really consider these definitions for himself. He told us that being responsible was a feeling, a duty, and an action. While being accountable was quite literally whether or not your feeling, duty, and action delivered the desirable result. Whether you, as the reader, agree or disagree, Gary now had clarity, and through clarity, he could have meaningful discussions with the people on his team and the stakeholders he collaborated with.

Making meaning is the underlying essence of everything in this book.

Meaningful leaders create meaningful organizations that deliver meaningful results. It's easy, lazy, and meaningless to simply accept words and actions at face value. Your objective is to become a master at making meaning, starting with yourself. Only then can you help create it for others and lead them to transform meaning from a concept into reality for themselves. When you commit to doing this, you are a step ahead of the vast majority of people out there trying to lead and manage well. Your legacy, impact, influence, results, and anything and everything in between will be determined by how clear you are about the type of leader you want to be.

Consider this book a leadership version of 'choose your own adventure.' At every twist and turn you face, you get to choose your next action. I'll nudge you in certain directions, I'll give you examples, studies, and opinions to help you choose with intention, but ultimately, the choice is always yours. Only you can decide how you make leadership meaningful for you.

GOOD LEADER, BAD LEADER

One of the first activities I have participants in our programs engage in is a discussion about good and bad leaders. I ask them to think about the best leader they've ever worked with and talk about the things this leader did and the qualities they demonstrated. Once all of that good, warm fluffy stuff is over, I ask them to do the same about the worst leader they've ever had. This seems to come very easy as people usually have several examples to pull from. You can really feel the energy shift as the corners of people's mouths turn downwards and they resentfully describe the damaging and dissonant leaders. Once we've had these two very different discussions, I display the contrast between the two. The visual below shows a common result of these conversations.

Best Leader	Worst Leader
Selfless	Ego
Curious	Poor communication
Gives autonomy	Have to do it 'their way'
Makes decisions	Emotionally volatile
Clear communication	Shames others
Predictable	Bully
Authentic/real	Know-it-all
Trusting	Takes credit/gives blame
Provides accountability and feedback	Micro-manager/controlling
Inspirational	Untrustworthy
Leads by example	Gossips
Compassionate but firm	Dismissive
Cheerleader/champion	Lacks self-awareness
Develops people	Lies
Empowering	Judgemental
Aligns people	Self-promoting
Removes obstacles	Doesn't listen

These columns show the most common attributes people articulate based on their best and worst experiences with leaders. Most people would agree that the qualities on the left are more desirable than the qualities on the right. If you are like me and can be really honest with yourself, you can look at the two columns and accept that you've done things on both sides as a leader, intentionally or unintentionally.

But now isn't the time to dwell on what you've done in the past. What's important here is to be aware of these contrasting qualities and understand what you can do to spend more time in the left column.

FORGET HIGH PERFORMANCE

There is a dark side in the fight for high performance when it's self-serving, short sighted and devoid of true meaning. In many organizations, high performance is designed to drive maximum shareholder value, making the rich richer while using people as pawns in the corporate game of thrones. Seeking promotions, reaching bonuses and claiming power are the main events of this gladiator showdown, and depending on where you sit, the show is either gory or glorious.

If this is what you came for, do the world a favor and put this book away. I totally get it. I've been trapped into playing the zero-sum game myself at times. That might be the way the world used to be, but truth be told, it doesn't fly anymore. We need fewer excessive personal profit maximizers and more meaning maximizers in positions of influence and at the helm of organizations. If personal profit maximization at the expense of others describes you and you're willing to change, then come on in and make yourself at home. But I'll warn you now, I'll challenge you on the things you say are important so you can get clear on what's really meaningful.

What I don't want you to think is that I reject high performance. I don't. I love the principles because they work. It's how people apply them that creates gross and unnecessary pain. Leaders who use high performance principles to extract more from their people to benefit their own bonus, or step on people as they themselves climb higher and achieve more—those are the people in the Bad Leader column. High performance can mask itself behind a world-changing vision while it squeezes more and more from its people, only to discard them when their executive forecasts go wrong. Pure high performance is highly transactional and discards people in pursuit of that shiny trophy or vanity metric. It's often a very short-term approach that hopes to yield lasting results through using a 'next man up' philosophy. Regardless of where you stand in this model, it usually ends with eroded relationships. Archaic high performance models put humanity second. Those who get it, understand there is an approach that can achieve great results through a meaning-driven, humanity first approach.

Meaning-driven leadership is not about slacking off, holding hands, and singing Kumbaya. It holds the same tension of any high performance model, yet offers a different, more intentional and meaningful entry point. As you work on defining the type of leader you want to be, I want you to develop some intentional operating procedures—helpful rules and tools to help you become grounded, consistent, and effective (We will work on this throughout the book and refine it in the last chapter). While I will be using high performance athletics principles, I want you to forget about being a high performance leader. High performance, while valiant and revered, isn't what's needed moving forward. The world needs something different and better than high performance leadership. What it needs are leaders committed to meaningful performance. This is the only thing that's going to transform work from being the place where people's hearts hurt the most into a place where people feel they can express themselves, feel valued, and make a meaningful impact in their world.

A meaning-driven leadership mindset and approach might take longer to build, but it leverages the power of compound interest. Leaders driven by meaning focus on creating conditions that are rich and fulfilling rather than reactionary and unforgiving. Meaningful leadership is about inspiring and growing your people instead of using, dismissing, and discarding them. These are the big things meaningful leaders do to create meaningful results, and that is what we will work on later in this book. To deliver big things however, it's the little things that matter most.

LITTLE THINGS, BIG IMPACT

Here's the great news. The solution to many of our problems in life and leadership often lie in the little things.

For almost 10 years I competed in the sport of bobsled, where a 100th of a second could make the difference between being on the podium or out of the race completely. Football is a game of inches where the spot of the ball, your timing, body position, or your reach on a single play can change the outcome of a game.

Success is determined by commitment, consistency, and practice. Exercising the little things that make the biggest difference. Do not get caught in the trap of the endless pursuit of the mystical magic bullet that will magically fix all of your leadership challenges. It is subtle but significant actions that will make the difference between creating critical momentum or a cancerous downward spiral inside your business. When it comes to cultivating talent, creating strong teams that deliver incredible value and cultures that take risks and demonstrate resilience, it's the little things leaders do or don't do that make the biggest difference. Decent leaders do the obvious things that need to be done. They do enough to get by and hope that results will follow suit. But leaders driven by purpose and meaning obsess about the tiny, almost invisible levers that create that critical momentum and inspire engagement to deliver results that matter.

Anyone can send a card on Valentine's day or take you for lunch on your birthday—those are easy. You don't have to think much about doing the easy things or grabbing the low-hanging fruit. But what do you do when times are tough? Or how do you create significant moments in a seemingly insignificant day? When you ask yourself this, you are on the track to meaningful leadership.

It doesn't matter to me what type of leader you were or are now. What matters most is whether or not you are willing to commit to being a meaningful performance leader moving forward. This book will help you do that if you are willing to focus on the little things that make a big difference.

CONCLUSION

Leadership is a word frequently used but woefully misunderstood, its meaning long lost in platitudes and clichés. As a leader, only you can define leadership for yourself in a meaningful way. Once you've done that, you're getting closer to discovering what the hell leadership is and how you deliver it.

In this chapter, I invited you to take a good look at yourself. Is your expertise or your toxic ego holding you or your team back? Are you victim to the vortex that keeps you in the spin cycle of unproductive homeostasis? Do you spend most of your time in the Bad Leader column? It's your job to take this exploration and create a meaningful and personal definition of leadership for yourself. Once you've done that, you can experiment and refine your approach, bypassing high performance as you step into something even better: meaningful performance. And meaningful performance starts with the little things—addressing little pains before they get bigger and taking consistent little actions that have long-term benefits.

This book is going to show you how. And the entry point is through our Science Behind Success™ model.

THINGS TO REMEMBER

- Three things that can hold you back as a leader: expertise, ego, and the vortex.
- The forgetting curve: you'll forget most of what you learn by the end of the day if you don't build structures for retention.
- There are many different definitions of leadership. What's most important is creating your own personal definition.
- What qualities did the best and worst leaders you've ever had embody?
- While leaders get caught in the endless pursuit of the magic bullet to their leadership problems, it's often the little things that make the biggest difference.
- Make meaningful performance your objective and use high performance tools to achieve it.

2

THE SCIENCE BEHIND SUCCESS™

By reading this book, you are going to answer that single burning question that keeps every leader awake at night…

How do I myelinate hypertrophic memes within my leadership epigenome?

At the end of this book, you will not only know what this means, but you'll know exactly how to do it, and why it matters.

For those of you creative types who might be overwhelmed by scientific terms—don't worry. You need not get overwhelmed by me being overly 'sciency'. But just in case, I'll translate the concept in a more digestible way for you:

You are about to find out how masochism, Tom Cruise, butterflies, and video games are going to change your life and the trajectory of your leadership and business.

But before we go skipping down the yellow brick road, let's get really clear about what I mean when I talk about the Science Behind Success™.

GOOD AND BAD SCIENCE

What do you think we mean when we say 'science'? To me, there is science at its best and science at its worst.

Let's travel to the bustling streets of a small town in Hungary in the 19th century. Imagine the jingle jangle of horse-drawn carriages and the rumble of wooden wheels over cobblestone. We swoop into the lab of a doctor named Ignaz Semmelweis.

In the 1840s, health science was not what it is today. A devastating disease called puerperal fever was taking its toll as the primary cause of death under childbearing women. Our Dr. Semmelweis obsessed over this problem and eventually found, what seemed to him, a slightly intuitive yet repeatable solution. His findings should have been celebrated as a revolutionary discovery, but instead they were laughed at and considered heresy because they were in conflict with the medical profession's beliefs at the time. In fact, his solution was so offensive to his peers that they ostracized him from their social circles. He was considered too 'simple'.

What was the crazy suggestion that was so offensive? Semmelweis found that doctors needed to wash their hands—a very simple thing that could yield significant results. But because medical 'experts' were committed to their beliefs at the time, Semmelweis's idea was discredited and dismissed. It wasn't until 20 years later when Louis Pasteur came up with the germ theory that the work of Semmelweis was actually accepted and recognized. How ironic is it that physicians, whom people counted on to save them, were in fact largely responsible for infecting them and causing them to die? Really consider this and how it applies to you. How often are you unable or unwilling to see or accept what you might be doing to infect the situations that challenge you the most? Remember that trail of crumbs?

When you make your experience the 'truth', you only accept ideas and solutions that confirm your current beliefs and biases. You make validating your ideas more important than the exploration of new insights and learning. You become more and more committed to your truth, your biases, your expertise, and all of the data you've collected throughout your career, and you dismiss anything outside of it. This blindness puts you and the people in your organization at risk.

Mark Twain nailed it when he wrote, "It's not what you don't know that will hurt ya. It's what you know fer sure that just ain't so."

Kodak is another notorious example of bad science bias. They were committed to their truth around their existing business model, which was entirely based on film photography. Despite the emerging and disruptive digital technology (which, ironically they invented themselves), they stuck to their guns and knew 'fer sure' that the future of film was more important and profitable than continuing to invest in the quixotic adventure of digital technology. The result of being committed to their expertise? A rapid decline that led to bankruptcy.

Look, we have to make strategic decisions with the best information we have in the moment, and we don't and won't always get it right. I've been guilty of several wrong ones—thankfully not at the scale of Kodak—but I have made several. The point is that we can get blinded by our biases, expertise, and current information, and this blindness can come at a significant cost.

Science is always changing. If you are reading this book expecting the 'truth' and direct correlation of each specific area of science and how it relates to standard performance metrics, you'll be disappointed. Maybe you'll even be outraged and want to chirp me relentlessly on Twitter (@ jayson_krause). So, take a deep breath and let's level set. What you won't get from this book is a detail-by-detail aspect of each area of science I introduce so you can optimize your physiology, biorhythms, and cognitive function. If you want to learn about how to lengthen your telomeres or maximize your mitochondria, I suggest reading *Super Human* by Dave Asprey, see a performance physiologist, or read some robust medical journals. I'm not even going to put in a small percentage of the studies that helped shape this book, because it's called cognitive overload—remember, you'll just forget most of it anyhow. What I will give you is enough science that will provide you greater insight into the mechanisms behind everything you need to know, and more importantly, I will give you the tools to apply it.

At its best, science is the pursuit of greater discovery. You obsess and become curious about the challenges in your environment and use that obsession to find better ways of doing what you do. Challenging your assumptions and defining what not to do are essential to being a meaningful leader. When you embrace this concept, you begin to identify the little things that can make the biggest difference instead of stepping over them and dismissing them as too simple, becoming your own cause of infection.

WHAT IS SUCCESS?

If science is considered 'the pursuit of greater understanding,' what do I mean when I say, success?

In your mind's eye, I want you to envision ultimate success. See it. Feel it rush over you like a toasty fever. What does it look like? How do you feel? How would you know you've achieved it? What are the first things that pop into your head?

If you're like many people, success might mean having all the time and money in the world to do what you want, when you want, in any way you can imagine, without a care in the world. You can simply sit back and focus on your favorite yoga pose in front of the Taj Mahal—another trophy on your Instagram feed.

While some might hold this as the ultimate vision of success, I consider it decay and atrophy. How I frame success is simple. Progression.

Success is a succession from where I was yesterday to where I am today. Growth, improvement, pain, development—whatever adjective you want to use. Success, as I view it, is the commitment to be better. To be clear, it's not about being perfect. It's about being better.

The alternative is to get caught in the powerful and seductive trap of destination-itis, where you bypass what's necessary today and dwell in the fantasy of a future story. A story you tell yourself of when you finally become VP, president, or CEO, or when you reach that IPO stage or sell your company—add whatever destination trap you want. Once you reach that destination, that fantasy you've created in your mind, *then* you will finally be successful.

It's all bullshit. I've had many clients who thought their lives would be better once they reached a certain milestone, only to realize, when they got there, that it was nothing like they thought it would be. Destination-itis is real. Too many people have felt the sharp pain of discovering they won a game they actually never wanted to play. Often, the result is empty disappointment that leaves you asking, now what?

Don't take this the wrong way. Vision is very important. The key is using it as an inspirational tool and compass. But when you allow any goal to become the illusion of being the finish line or the truth, you're setting yourself up for disaster. If the goal is your finish line, it can easily become the anvil you drag along for the rest of your life, constantly pointing to who you were instead of re-labelling that milestone as a mile-marker towards a truly meaningful journey. As the famous saying goes, "When you reach the top of a mountain, keep climbing."

If science is the pursuit of greater discovery, then success is using that discovery to get better. Every day. In service of something greater than your bonus or promotion.

LET'S TALK CONTEXT

If content is king, context is the kingdom.

When I observe leaders in meetings or team situations, the content of their communication is usually pretty good. What they often miss, though, is providing the deeper context surrounding strategy, situations, and decisions. Context is the background environment that determines the quality of life your content has. How it lives and breathes, or whether it falls flat on its face. Context is extremely important and can significantly change the way people receive information and act on it.

Carol Dweck is a brilliant professor of psychology out of Stanford who is known for her work around mindset. In one of her famous studies, Dweck split a Grade 5 class in half and taught each group something different. The teachers didn't know what she was doing with each group. When the children were put back into the classroom, the teachers noticed demonstrable behavioral changes in the students from one of the groups. They were engaging in a completely different way than they used to. Rather than become overwhelmed by the challenge of learning something new in the classroom, one group of students demonstrated more curiosity, resilience, and proactivity in how they embraced the problems presented to them. What did she teach this group of students?

Simple. Dweck taught the first group a standard science class. They absorbed the learning and went back to the class as if it was a normal classroom event. To the second group she taught some basic brain science—a simplified lesson on the neural mechanisms behind learning: what happens to the brain during learning, how does it grow, and how you can influence that growth? This information provided them with more context around why their teacher challenged them while they learned and what happens in the brain when things are hard. It answered a lot of questions that otherwise would have taken both time and cognitive energy as students invariably asked, why are we doing this? The students changed their perspective on themselves and their learning environment because they gained deeper understanding through context.

Context provides a level of clarity that enables people to focus on what matters. This not only works with young children through school, but is also really important in leadership and management, especially when it comes to developing meaningful relationships, and is a vital underlying principle of the Science Behind Success™ method.

THE SCIENCE BEHIND SUCCESS™ METHOD

Famous scientist Thomas Kuhn wrote, "You can understand anything once you have the metaphor to perceive it." Metaphors are powerful devices of exploration and discovery. They often lead to greater understanding and context, enabling you to take meaningful action.

The four pillars of science of our Science Behind Success™ model act as a metaphor for you to understand yourself as a leader. The model illustrates the different elements and the key steps that will help you on this transformational journey as you grow to understand yourself and your environment. Over time, through continuous exercise and long-term commitment to the process, these principles will become an essential part of your leadership practice, helping you accelerate and achieve meaningful leadership and performance.

The four principles of science that underpin the Science Behind Success™ model are:

Hypertrophy: Understanding growth and mindset

Memetics: The viral power of words and behaviors inside your business

Epigenetics: The little things that create or kill your culture

Myelin: Developing the habits of a meaningful leader

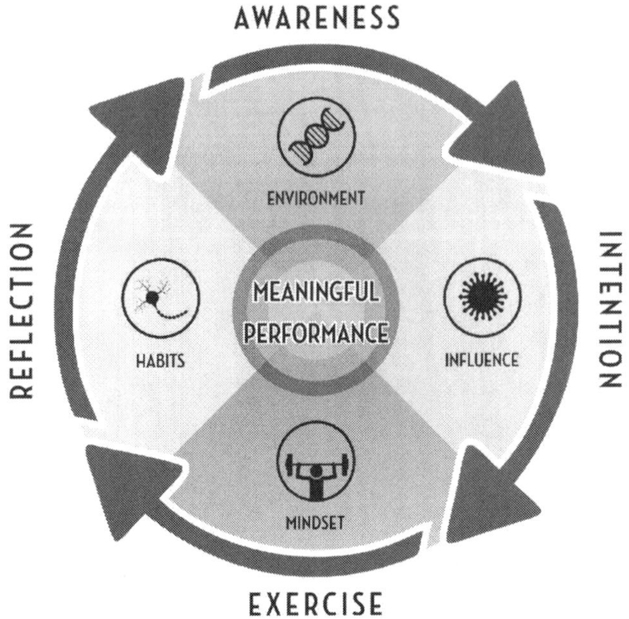

The Science Behind Success™ Model

Together, the four words on the outside of our model create an important equation:

A+I+E+R = A+

Awareness + Intention + Exercise + Reflection = Increased Awareness

These four steps will help you to rapidly elevate your awareness. When you develop better awareness as a leader, you can transform that awareness into actions that create impact that matters to you, the people around you, and your business.

British journalist Miles Kington said that, "Knowledge is knowing that a tomato is a fruit; wisdom is not putting it in a fruit salad." Knowledge is everywhere, and yet the world is starving for wisdom. The Science Behind Success™ model is designed to accelerate the conversion of awareness into wisdom, so you can stop telling people that tomatoes should technically be in a fruit salad. People don't care. Just get the right ingredients that make a great fruit salad.

Taking leaders through the four steps of the Science Behind Success™ model accelerates the acquisition of wisdom so they can deliver meaningful performance.

STEP 1: AWARENESS

The first step in upping your leadership game is to seek to constantly elevate your awareness of yourself and your environment. Awareness is the entry point to any type of meaningful transformation. If you aren't open to it, you won't gain awareness and will likely remain entrenched in the old thoughts, patterns, and behaviors and keep infecting the things that you are trying to cure.

There are multiple opportunities every day to exercise your awareness muscle. Think about the last time you experienced something that gave you greater awareness about yourself or your business. It could be something as simple as an interaction, podcast, or a learning event. It could be something bigger and painful like a mistake that led to losing a primary customer, a key employee resigning, a technology that made you or your business obsolete, or perhaps even the loss of a loved one.

Whatever the event or challenge, big or small, you can use it to elevate your awareness. Awareness is the first critical part of the cycle.

STEP 2: INTENTION

The second part of the cycle is intention. Once they've experienced an event that elevates their awareness, great leaders use that awareness to reinforce or reshape their intention.

Let's break this down using an example. Say an employee surprises me by abruptly resigning.

Awareness: A key employee gives me her notice. I was completely blindsided, hurt, and frankly, angry. Rather than blame her for being entitled, I reflect on my responsibility. What I can accept is that I didn't give her much recognition or support, and I simply assumed she was happy.

Intention: I could label this as circumstantial or blame her for thinking the grass is greener, or I can really embrace what I'm responsible for and become intentional about how I engage and recognize the people on my team. My intention will be to put a sharp focus on recognizing the contributions of my team members.

STEP 3: EXERCISE

The third part of our model is perhaps the most difficult. Exercise. Intentions don't mean a damn thing on their own if we don't put the intention into action. You have to commit to a specific structure and engage in the process of delivering your intention. It's an exercise. Let's return to the same example of our team member who resigns.

Awareness: A key employee gives me her notice. I was completely blindsided, hurt, and frankly, angry. Rather than blame her for being entitled, I reflect on my responsibility. What I can accept is that I didn't give her much recognition or support, and I simply assumed she was happy.

Intention: I could label this as circumstantial or blame her for thinking the grass is greener, or I can really embrace what I'm responsible for and become intentional about how I engage and recognize the people on my team. My intention will be to put a sharp focus on recognizing the contributions of my team members.

Exercise: I will focus on identifying at least one thing this week that I can recognize each team member for. (In Chapter 5, I will give you very specific tools that will transform your ability to partner with others through engineering your relationships.)

STEP 4: REFLECTION

If the third part of the model is the most difficult, the fourth part is where most people fail miserably. Reflection. This is where you take a step back and assess yourself—the delta between the impact you had and the impact you wanted to have. This is where you get to identify what worked, what didn't work, and what's next. Just like an athlete will watch a video and analyze their technique and how they responded to a situation, you will do the same thing with a critical eye so you can be better prepared to deliver excellence the next time you face something similar.

Awareness: A key employee gives me her notice. I was completely blindsided, hurt, and frankly, angry. Rather than blame her for being entitled, I reflect on my responsibility. What I can accept is that I didn't give her much recognition or support, and I simply assumed she was happy.

Intention: I could label this as circumstantial or blame her for thinking the grass is greener, or I can really embrace what I'm responsible for and become intentional about how I engage and recognize the people on my team. My intention will be to put a sharp focus on recognizing the contributions of my team members.

Exercise: I will focus on identifying at least one thing this week that I can recognize each team member for.

Reflection: I was able to find something to recognize each member for, but some of them were rushed. I forgot about capturing the moments and struggled to find something meaningful for a few of them. Next week I will make sure to capture a quick note at the end of the day so I can deliver better quality recognition.

Most people would agree that experience is the greatest teacher. Yet most people fail to really take the time to reflect on their micro-challenges and successes each day to leverage the learning and accelerate wisdom. Because you're reading this book, I'm confident that you aren't one of those people. Even if you are, I believe that this will change after you read this book, embrace the structure it provides, and apply the principles to your leadership practice. Just like an athlete analyzes a video and obsesses over what is working and what needs to be tweaked, you'll learn to immerse yourself in a model that creates deeper meaning and will truly accelerate your effectiveness as a leader.

PRACTICE MAKES PROGRESS

The Science Behind Success™ model is an invitation to step into the process of seeking greater understanding so you can grow and deliver greater meaning into your life and business. This pursuit can be achieved through activating awareness so you can become more intentional in your style and approach. Of course, intentions don't mean anything on their own.

I'm going to tell you what upsets me. During a past program of ours, when the first module was over and we were starting the second module, the group was discussing the application of some of the tools they had learned. During this discussion, one of our students said, "They really didn't do anything for me." This is where my face goes red and my angry dad voice kicks in, just like when my son asks me where his jacket is while he's wearing muddy boots and standing on top of it.

I'll say the same thing to you as I did to him, minus the red face and dad voice. The tools will do nothing if you don't use the tools. Just like hammers don't build houses, sinks don't clean dishes, and money doesn't invest itself. Exercise, reflect, and get better information for yourself so you can make better choices and engage in better exercises.

There are no magic bullets, and I'm not claiming this book is one. But I promise you it will completely shift the trajectory of your career and your business if you absorb it with a beginner's mind, truly immerse yourself in the questions, and commit to exercising what thousands of leaders around the world have. Identify specific ways you can exercise so you can complete the loop and reflect to keep the flywheel spinning in service of your growth. The questions at the end of each chapter are important. They will help guide you through this process and get you multiple reps in using this model.

CONCLUSION

Science is the pursuit of greater understanding. It's about experimenting and learning. If you are curious and willing to step into the laboratory of your leadership, you will gain valuable insight to help you achieve success—to be better, grow, and deliver meaning into your work.

The Science Behind Success™ model can help you on this transformational journey. The metaphors of hypertrophy, epigenetics, memetics, and myelin provide the context to understand your influence and power as a leader in an organization, and how you can use that power for good. Exercising the principles of the Science Behind Success™ model requires that you learn to activate awareness, become more intentional, and then exercise and experiment with that intention. When you reflect on your experience and seek to learn more, you'll unlock the next level of awareness, and before you know it, you'll be so much better and faster than you ever imagined.

But reading this book and dipping your toe in the Science Behind Success™ model is only the beginning. It's up to you to begin practicing its principles and to make it work. Nothing works if you don't make it work for you.

THINGS TO REMEMBER

- Honor Ignaz Semmelweis and wash your hands.
- How might you be infecting the problems you are trying to solve?
- Most of your leadership challenges are as simple as washing your hands – just not easy.
- 'Science' is the pursuit of greater understanding. Be committed to learning more than the validation of your own ideas.
- Hold the term 'Success' as progression (am I better today than yesterday?).
- Awareness + Intention + Exercise + Reflection = Greater Awareness.

CREATE MEANING

Awareness: What are three things you are doing/not doing in your organization that are infecting the problems you are trying to solve?

Intention: What can you do to be intentional about the actions you identified in the question above?

Exercise: Specify how you will act on a daily basis to counter this infection.

Reflect: Schedule time in your calendar to reflect on these problems again, track your progress, and identify new ones.

3

MEANINGFUL MASOCHISM

After I retired from my international bobsledding career in 2006, I went through a paradoxical transformation. I was experiencing the incredible pain of uncertainty, failure, and transitioning into the unknown, but I also felt a strange sense of liberation. I had been liberated from my own harsh expectations, the expectations of my coaches, and the perceived expectations of those who supported me along my athletic journey. During this transformation I dabbled in a few different things. I volunteered in the war zone in Northern Uganda and went on a personal journey of discovery, all of it due to the disruptive experience of not qualifying for a spot in the 2006 Olympics.

Having spent eight years of my life in a weight room as an athlete, one of my goals in my post-sport career was to never lift a weight again. I wanted to stay fit and healthy in other ways, but my joints and muscles hurt from years of lifting heavy weights. I would have been happy to never see a weight room ever again in my entire life. However, after about a year without any type of weight training, my close friend and 2010 Olympic champion, Steve Mesler (there he is again), convinced me to come do a workout with the boys. Despite my vow to never lift again, I did miss the community that came with pushing myself in a training group and decided to join them and just mess around a bit. Now, when you're with a group of high performance athletes, there is no such thing as messing around. I quickly found myself trying to lift the type of weights I could in my prime—pushing myself had been encoded deeply into my operating system, and I was soon grunting and straining in ways I hadn't in the previous 12 months.

On this day, I was under the bench press, pushing up a weight, fighting to create the force needed to accelerate the weight faster. On my last repetition, my body couldn't do it, and the weight fell slowly onto my chest. Steve helped lift the weight back onto the rack and playfully smacked my shoulder. "Perfect," he said, "exactly where you want to end. Failure."

I instantly started reflecting on what he had said. The clouds split apart as I came to a realization. Life seemed to finally make sense, the reasons behind all my failures and successes revealed.

As an athlete, I knew that my objective, every day, was to push my body to reach that point of failure. That one final core exercise that produced the burning pain that forced me to collapse. One more squat, one more lift…that was the recipe for getting better. THE recipe.

That got me thinking. If this was required for my body to get better and stronger, then why did I retreat from the space of failure in so many other areas of my life? Many of my relationships had me walking on eggshells. In driving a bobsleigh, I had definitely operated in a place of avoiding failure, even steering clear (no pun intended) from simple mistakes at all costs. I avoided failure in so many things outside of my physiology, and as a result, stunted my growth in those areas.

In that moment with Steve, I realized that the secret to all growth lay in simple physiological realities. The more you understand and apply the key elements of growth, the more rapid and effective that growth can be.

Transforming yourself and your business starts with hypertrophy.

In this chapter I will take you through the first principle of the Science Behind Success™ model: mindset and hypertrophy. Struggle and resistance are necessary for growth, and how you use this principle, both as a mindset and practice, will differentiate you from a below average performer. This is important to how you shape your mind as a leader and engage with the inherent stress that comes with leading the most challenging thing in the world—people. How you engage with the pains in your environment—how you exercise them like muscles—will truly determine the strength, resilience, agility, and dynamic power you possess as a leader.

YOU CHOOSE YOUR 'TROPHY'

When it comes to growth, all roads lead to hypertrophy. Most of us are more familiar with this process through the common saying, no pain, no gain. This simply means that when a muscle is subjected to stress or resistance, it adapts by growing.

Hypertrophy is that feeling you get after a hard workout that leaves you in slight (or sometimes severe) agony. Simplified, it's the stress you put your muscles under that creates micro-tears in the tissue. Your muscles respond by growing stronger, so you are better equipped to handle the next, possibly more rigorous workout.

The quickest way to achieve hypertrophy in your muscles is by purposefully engaging in the stress and resistance in your environment so you can accelerate growth. This is why you go to the gym, hop on your Peloton, or pop in that old VHS and gleefully sweat to the oldies with Richard Simmons—you create opportunities of pain and discomfort because you are in pursuit of a vision of a healthy and energetic lifestyle.

The opposite of hypertrophy is atrophy. Atrophy is the gradual decline in effectiveness or vigor due to underuse or neglect. Instead of engaging in the deliberate and difficult process of struggle and pain, you acquiesce or avoid the struggles in your environment. This leads to an atrophy of function, loss of ability, and a decrease in fitness. Physiologically, atrophy is a real and present danger, and it translates into how you lead and whether you choose to engage or retreat from the challenges in your role.

When you get seduced into comfort and ease, certain skills can and will atrophy. You gradually become incapable of handling certain things, you lose confidence, and your resourcefulness and willpower eventually plunge. As a result, you might end up leaving your position for an easier and better situation. The atrophy plunge is so strong that you become an organizational parasite, sucking the nutrients from others, marching lifelessly from office to office like an atrophied zombie. All because you wouldn't embrace the challenges in your world.

So what is the difference between those who embrace and engage in the process of career and leadership hypertrophy and those who commit to atrophy? The simple answer is mindset. Everything you do cascades from your mindset.

GROWTH MINDSET

The term growth mindset is used frequently across industries, but what does it mean?

Carol Dweck (our Stanford professor from Chapter 2) authored an excellent book on the topic—*Mindset*[7]—which I believe should be required reading for every teacher, coach, and parent.

In one of her famous studies with fifth graders, Dweck illustrated how a single sentence of praise (six words) could stimulate growth or fixed mindsets, making up to a 50% difference in performance.

Dweck gave each child a basic, level-one test that consisted of fairly easy puzzles. After completing the test (in which all of them did well), she informed each child of their scores individually, adding a single sentence of praise.

---

7 Dweck, C. (2016). *Mindset: The New Psychology of Success*. Ballantine Books.

Half were praised for intelligence: "You must be smart at this."

Half were praised for effort: "You must have worked really hard."

After receiving this praise, the fifth graders were tested a second time, but this time they were offered a choice between taking a harder test and an easier test. Shockingly, 90% of the kids who were praised for their effort chose to take the harder test, while the majority of kids praised for their natural intelligence chose the easier test.

When tested a third time—with the same, much harder test for everyone—none of the kids did well. When the children were asked about the third test afterwards, the group initially praised for their effort said they liked it and really got involved with exercising solutions and strategies. But the group that was initially praised for their natural intelligence said they hated it and took it as proof that they weren't smart after all.

The final step of the study returned to a level-one test of fairly basic puzzles. The results of this last step were quite telling. The children praised for effort improved their initial scores by 30%, whereas the scores of those praised for natural intelligence declined by 20%. Dweck was so surprised that she ran the study five more times. The result was the same every single time.

Why did this happen?

The words people say to us teach us where to focus our attention. In the case of this study, the focus was put on either the variables the kids could control (in this case effort), or on something outside of their control—natural ability.

A growth mindset is the ability to focus on the variables you can control and long-term progress. Individuals with a fixed mindset, on the other hand, allow themselves to get seduced into instant gratification, present bias, and the ego-driven illusion of displaying perfection. Those who hold on tightly to a fixed mindset judge themselves and others as if the finish line is right now, in this moment. Everything, including themselves, is on one side of the line: good or bad, smart or stupid. When push comes to shove and the stakes get high, those with a fixed mindset are likely to sneak off into the shadows in the hopes of preserving their false image of perfection.

Growth mindset and fixed mindset can be explained simply (ok, relatively simply) through biology or physics.

According to Dr. Bruce Lipton, a cellular biologist at Stanford, survival requires protection as well as growth. However, cells cannot be in both modes at once. Remaining in the protection mode will eventually destroy the body's defenses because normal replacement of protein parts cannot be continued, eventually resulting in various diseases. Similarly, in line with Einstein's general relativity theory, space-time containing matter cannot remain stationary and must either expand or contract.

So when you consider Lipton and Einstein, you have to ask yourself, am I habitually driven by growth or protection? Am I expanding or contracting?

When Steve and I delivered the very first version of the Science Behind Success™ program to MBA students at the University of Florida, one of the professors told us that MBA students often get into GPA protection mode—they do things by the book seeking to preserve their grade and status. While this helps them meet their short term goals of graduating and ranking, it often sets them back in the long-term as it gets them into a difficult-to-escape fixed mindset they unintentionally end up taking into the workforce. Similarly, new leaders can be paralyzed by the new requirements of managing and leading and can easily get sucked back into what validates them, which is doing the work themselves.

A growth mindset liberates you from fear-based preservation mode and present bias of 'right now'. It is a difficult but important task for leaders to shed their ego, let go of being 'the best', and rather work towards exercising 'their best'. Embracing the physiological requirements for growth that lead to long-term and meaningful results is essential in building strong, meaningful leadership.

TWO TYPES OF GROWTH

There are two types of hypertrophy: Sarcoplasmic and myofibrillar. Each demonstrates a different path to growth, and you and your organization likely have taken one or the other.

Sarcoplasmic hypertrophy is what bodybuilders train. They grow the outer fascia of the muscles to be big and look good. The bigger you get, the more resources and work it takes to maintain the size and stay big. There isn't much of a correlation to functional strength as you get bigger, and with this type of training, bodybuilders tend to be big but slow and less functional. The objective is more about optics—you train to look good. Some seek to accelerate their growth curve by injecting steroids or HGH (growth hormones) so they can achieve their growth goals faster.

Metaphorically, companies can unintentionally fall into the same growth strategy. They fall victim to the belief that bigger is better. They throw resources at everything so they can grow more, faster. Finally, they reach a tipping point of diminishing returns. They lose any evidence of being dynamic, have little to no agility to respond to external stimuli, and eventually can't maintain the injection of resources and energy to sustain themselves. This forces them to pull back, leaving them flabby and ineffective, living in the past.

Myofibrillar hypertrophy is different. This is when you strengthen the contractile proteins instead of the outer fascia. You train to be explosive (think Olympic weightlifter or sprinter). You train to be dynamic, agile, explosive…all of those things. You train to specifically be good at something. The goal is not necessarily to look good. The important thing here is that the core is strong and the contractile proteins are explosive. You resist the urge to simply look like you were chiseled from stone, but make your proteins a critical mechanism to break through barriers and deliver results. It takes longer, requires a strong foundation, and is more sustainable and easier to activate even after periods of low training cycles.

Great leaders take the same approach to how they lead others and grow a strong, sustainable team and business. Along with building their own strong, personal foundation, they find ways to strengthen the contractile proteins within their business. They develop and strengthen their people to be dynamic high performers. They tend not to throw money at unneeded mercenaries or invest in resume builders to simply fill a quick gap while they pursue an unsustainable growth curve.

What kind of growth inspires you more? Your ego naturally loves the optics and attention that comes with sarcoplasmic growth. But true meaning-driven leaders strive for myofibrillar hypertrophy, building something that matters, fiber by fiber—something that transcends their quarterly report or even their career.

So how do you cultivate a mindset for lasting, meaningful growth? There are three aspects of growth mindset in particular that I want you to hold closely and embrace like a dear friend. These concepts can make the difference between leadership hypertrophy and the atrophy of despair. They are deviance, masochism, and simulation.

DEVIANCE

Deviance? Won't that get me thrown in jail? Hold on.

I'll admit, I regularly skipped classes in college, but there was one class that sucked me in when my sociology professor said something so profound that it led me to keep attending. He said, "Deviance breeds innovation." He went on to talk about how when criminals break the law, they force the justice system to respond and be better. This principle pretty much sums up the necessary entry point in the cycle of pain-inflicted individual and organizational innovation.

Any type of deviance invites an opportunity to innovate. A deviation from what you intend, expect, or depend on is an indicator that something needs to be built, changed, or reinforced.

You either drive innovation through being deviant or something deviant forces you to innovate abruptly. What side would you rather be on? Unforeseen deviance will undoubtedly force you to innovate, but in my experience, leaders decrease the suffering that comes with unexpected and forced innovation when they already have a practiced mindset of deviance.

When you embrace deviance by examining and breaking the rules that you've developed—the ones that may have kept you and your business safe so far—you can create the next version of who you are, challenge what you do, and the way you do it. To be deviant is the practice of constantly challenging the way you do things and not blindly accepting the seductive easy street. You either engage in positive and periodic deviance that elevates your awareness, or you fall into a slumber and wait for a nightmare to wake you up and force you to scramble and innovate from a disadvantageous position.

Some common nightmares that push leaders into a state of forced innovation include:

- You assume your people are happy, but out of nowhere, a key leader leaves your team to join another organization. This painful departure leaves a huge hole and it takes a ton of work to get someone else up to speed.
- A disruptive technology makes what you do irrelevant and now you are holding on to what seems like a sinking ship.
- You lose a major account to a competitor, and all of a sudden you are in recovery mode.
- Your industry is hit hard by socio-political factors and your costs rise significantly, making it much more difficult to make a profit and keep the doors open.
- A big mistake reveals you haven't exercised the people skills necessary to provide strong direction, give straight feedback, and hold people accountable.
- A pandemic forces you to lead your whole business remotely as people practice self-distancing, and you aren't prepared to deliver the value your customers need and want.

All of these situations could rock you and force you to drastically change your leadership approach, business model, or even life. You either meet the stress and resistance and exercise what's needed for you to innovate, deviate, and respond to the environment differently, or you atrophy and die. Two possible outcomes, and of course, many versions of something in between.

One of my favorite examples of deviance can be demonstrated through the story of Joe Hill, the man who melted his silver spoon into a spartan space of self-inflicted pain to pursue a rugged and relentless path towards his dream.

Imagine being born into what others would look at as a perfect situation. You have all that you could ever want. Financial resources and a network of industry connections at your fingertips, a quick and easy launchpad for a fast career trajectory. Would you take it? Who wouldn't!? Most people would, but not Joe Hill. Joe gave all these seductive low hanging fruit the Heisman stiff-arm, as he was determined to plant and create his own orchard of organic and non-GMO-grown fruit—metaphorically of course.

Joe wanted to be a writer, and he wanted to be a good one. He had all of the conditions in place to set him up for instant easy-street success. But Joe didn't take it. He refused all of it. This career deviant was committed to perfecting his craft, and so he deliberately engaged in the hard work and adaptation required to be a better writer as he got rejected by publishers again and again. Not even Joe's writing agent and publisher knew who he actually was until he became a best seller. It wasn't until after he had a strong following of readers and had clearly established himself as a professional that the cat came out of the bag.

Joe Hill was none other than Joe Hillström King, the son of the world-famous author, Stephen King.

Fighting the seductive trap that comes with the illusion of instant success, Joe had the mentorship and mindset to be deviant and see the bigger picture. He was more committed to the craft of meaning and excellence than the illusion of overnight success.

The quicker the path you take to success, the higher the likelihood that you've built your empire on a house of cards. It can fall apart as quickly as it rose. Foundations take time, and foundations are hard work.

Building something that lasts takes sweat. It likely results in some form of mental and physical pain—probably both. But the deviant understands and accepts that deliberately creating our own pain can positively impact our growth and development.

MEANINGFUL MASOCHISM

Deviance requires purposeful masochism. I'll shoot straight. You are a masochist. If you aren't right now, I want you to be one.

Purposeful masochism is intentionally creating and engaging in the pain in pursuit of your vision. The opposite is stepping away from the fire, stepping away from the edge of discomfort, and the most common, stepping away from the pain of annoyance—why don't they get it!?

What happens when you step away? You got it, atrophy, or infection… or both.

Purposeful masochists passionately engage with the pain because they see it as an essential obstacle or a critical exercise on the path to becoming better. As Ryan Holiday, modern day philosopher says, "The obstacle is the way."

You are likely already a masochist in some ways.

In what areas of your life have you made things more difficult or deliberately engaged with pain to pursue something important to you? The obvious one is sweating and grunting and punishing your body in high-intensity interval training because you want to feel good and be a beast. Or, you painfully push away that molten chocolate cake for a healthier choice like blended broccoli. You get cut, scratched up, and covered in mud as you crawl on the ground and jump over fire with your friends in outdoor obstacle events like the Spartan race. Perhaps you make the difficult choice of saying no to spending money on the non-essentials of your business so you can be financially healthy and run a balanced budget. Maybe you commit to the discomfort that comes with giving direct and honest feedback so your people can get better. You are more committed to their growth than you are to being liked by them. There are many examples of where you likely engage in the difficult and painful processes so you can be healthy, fit, and endure the turbulence or greater stress that waits around the corner.

As a leader, it is a common and painful exercise to fight the urge to swoop in and helicopter fix everything. It's painful to watch someone struggle at something that would take you only five minutes to complete with the quality you want and need it. Instead, you're stuck watching as Bambi struggles to get up and walk when you want her to run the Kentucky Derby.

Do you engage with the pain of pausing your pace to grow others or succumb to being an easy street cape-donning expert?

The way you engage with pain will depend on how you see it. The trick is to reframe pain. Purposeful masochists-reframe what pain is. As Viktor Frankl, the famous psychologist who got stripped of everything and everyone in his life while being locked up in a Nazi war camp said, "Pain is inevitable, suffering is not."

Reframing pain is practicing the art of replacing your initial and possibly damaging perceptions with something more resourceful so you can get intentional and energized. Intentional and energized you say? Yes, this is the ultimate version of deviance and masochism, enabling you to see pain as a critical stepping stone in your development and the impact you make in your world. It is the ultimate expression of growth mindset.

There are two types of stress that largely influence whether or not you intentionally engage with pain and facilitate hypertrophy, or avoid it and atrophy. How you frame the pain or obstacle will greatly influence how you engage with it. Leaders who can link the pain to something meaningful experience eustress, while leaders who focus only on the downside of the pain are affected by distress. Guess which one is more likely to elicit creative expression and likely a better outcome?

Eustress: I am excited about destroying my body in pursuit of X, Y, or Z results. Or, I can see the value of retracting our business and taking a hit in revenue so that we can be better, more agile, and create more value for our clients. I see the opportunity that comes with social distancing forcing us to work as a distributed team. It's not easy, but where you focus your energy determines your level of enthusiasm and resourcefulness.

Distress: The illusion that the world is falling apart. The short-term thinking that this acute pain will last forever and is something to run away from, something that is bad and that you are unable to deal with. It's a significant irritation that I hope will go away. Distress is draining and creates a less resourceful you. Over time, it leads to the atrophy plunge.

A good leader and purposeful masochist can take a stressful or painful situation and reframe it into something meaningful. By doing so, your perspiration comes from inspiration instead of suffering. It's a simple process, it's just not easy.

PAIN AND SIMULATION

Why does leadership have to be so hard? So many people think they want to be leaders inside their business but quickly find out how challenging it is. Very few actually lead well, because leadership can be painful. As a meaningful masochist, you need to learn to use pain as the key unit of propulsion to your growth as a leader.

When I was starting my career as a leadership coach, I did a lot of research on building better people, better talent, and better leaders. I interviewed a vast number of people, hoping to uncover hidden leadership gems on building strong, confident, and productive people capable of catapulting organizations forward. One of those interview gems was Mr. S.—by all accounts, a successful man—who, despite being in his nineties and having nearly a century of knowledge, was still deeply committed to learning. "I have a goal of finishing all of the great books written in this world," he told me. "I still have so many to read, so I'd better stick around for a while!" We spoke about the business world's challenges, and one of the questions I asked him was, "If there is one thing we can do to build better, more capable leaders, what is it?" "More simulated arduous experiences," he answered without pause. I dug deeper, asking for more. "Everything is simulated," he explained. "We get caught up in things being so important, we treat them as the single biggest events of our lives. We become paralyzed with fear, compromising our values when we are overwhelmed, and the truth is, in most cases…they don't really matter. What matters is learning and being better after each experience." Intrigued by this insight, I dug even further while processing my past experiences in my mind, nodding my head at those numerous instances that matched Mr. S's leadership parable. He continued, "Once we understand that everything is essentially a simulation, preparing us for the next day, we can seek arduous circumstances that stretch and exercise our capabilities. The more we seek these or the more we create these for the people we care about most, the more we are developing capable and confident people."

But then it dawned on me.

"What about too many arduous experiences?" I asked. Again, without pause, Mr. S responded. "Don't throw someone to the wolves and leave them there. Let them know you're there. You won't take care of them, but you're there to catch them and help them grow," he explained. "When people experience the pain of failure or the discomfort of stress, that's important information they can learn from." He also spoke about how these situations relate to confidence and compassion. "When people have arduous experiences, they understand pain and struggle, therefore they're better able to put themselves in others' shoes," he said. "This builds compassion, empathy, and confidence…because they've been challenged before and they understand the traits and behaviors that can get them through these situations."

This interview has influenced the way I parent, how I view my own business leadership, and, of course, the programs we use to build meaningful leaders at Level 52.

What Mr. S said captures one of the critical leadership mindsets I cultivate with our business clients: the physiological reality that no pain means no gain. When you intentionally pursue the pain necessary to grow and develop, you become a more fit, capable, and confident leader over time. It's simple, but not easy. Whether you tried to deliver hard feedback, stood up for yourself or your team in front of your peers, or made a big presentation and failed. It's okay. It's all a simulation that you can learn from and use to be better for the next time.

BLIND SPOTS

Even when actively engaging in the daily simulations of leadership, it's easy to sometimes miss important information that could help you pivot your approach. Often you get early indicators and just choose not to do anything about it. Eventually, something significant happens and you're forced to react quickly.

While parking one day, I pulled into a multi-level parking structure and decided to back into the stall to make for an easier getaway at the end of the day. Halfway into the stall, the indicator started beeping so I looked at the screen showing what was behind my bumper. It looked as though I had five to six feet to go still before the rear parking block. Ignoring the intensifying beeping, I continued moving backwards with my eyes sharply focused on the camera. I kept going with confidence until finally my back window shattered against a cement block sticking out from the level above me. The sensor had identified the block, but I chose to ignore it because the camera didn't show it. This is an important metaphor. How often do you disregard indicators and rationalize why you are right and they are wrong?

This is why it's so important for leaders to actively seek out and have their blind spots revealed. Incredibly uncomfortable, yes, but immeasurably valuable. I believe a vital tool to elevate a leader's awareness is to go through a 360-feedback process where peers provide feedback on what they love and what they don't love about their leader. This process can shine a light on their potentially dangerous blind spots, providing early and strong indicators that enable them to make adjustments where needed.

If you are too focused on seeing things for yourself, it can lead to something getting damaged at the hands of our responsibility. It happens. It's what you do in that moment everything shatters that matters most. You can be victimized by it, or you can create from it.

OBJECT OR AGENT?

As humans, we have a distinct advantage, or at least it appears we do, to have conscious thought. To reflect on the past, live in the present, and plan for the future. How you use this gift of consciousness as a leader will determine whether you get dragged down by past failures, overcome by current pain, or overwhelmed by the perceived challenges ahead of you. Through the right mindset (and support) you get to decide if the current events will be something that are done to you, or if you'll grab the wheel, meet the simulation head-on, and lead your ship.

I was once coaching a CEO that was on the verge of selling his business. There were multiple parties at the table that were willing to invest a 10-figure amount to purchase the company from the CEO. But then it was revealed that a little item had been overlooked that put the entire deal at risk. As a result, one of the buying parties lowered their offer significantly. The next day, I met with the company's leaders in their boardroom to help them navigate the issue. The CEO came into the meeting both deflated and angry as hell. He sat there with a blank stare on his face, one hand grabbing his hair as he hung his head. How could this mistake have been missed!? "We just fucked up what could have been a historic deal. This mistake could end up losing us hundreds of millions of dollars. On top of that, now everyone is finger-pointing and we are scrambling to keep the other party at the table."

Question for the reader: Play armchair leader here and look through the lens of a simulation. The immediate evaluation of your own pain is rarely accurate, so in this case, what's the first pain that needed to be dealt with here?

The way I saw it, the first item that needed to be addressed was the blame and finger-pointing that was causing additional and unnecessary distress. Whatever happened, whatever was missed, whoever was responsible for the mishap—this was all irrelevant at that point. In such a situation, you need to take all of the energy that's being given to blame and finger-pointing and put it somewhere else. How might you do that?

I asked the CEO to imagine what he'd want his child to do in that situation—a young professional who was making her mark in her career. Imagine she was leading a business and had an oversight that led to a potentially tremendous mistake. How would he want her to respond?

"I'd want her to own it and take the steps necessary to fix it."

"Great. So, the first thing you are going to do after this is get the leadership team together and take responsibility for what happened."

"Okay, I can do that."

"Now, let's look at the assumptions causing the distress. Who says you have to make a deal today?"

"Well, it's the deadline we've given them."

"Okay, but who says you HAVE to make the deal today? Based on how the business is performing, I'd own the mistake, tell them you're taking it off the market, and let them know you'd love for them to re-engage if and when you put it back on the block. And, from what I've seen from you, it's simply going to cost them more money to get you next year. Don't let assumptions pull you into doing something you'll regret."

He sat back and absorbed this, and I shared the old parable of Maybe so, Maybe not. It goes something like this:

> *A farmer and his son had a beloved horse who helped the family earn a living. One day, the horse ran away and their neighbors exclaimed, "Your horse ran away; what terrible luck!" The farmer replied, "Maybe so, maybe not."*
>
> *A few days later, the horse returned home, leading a few wild horses back to the farm as well. The neighbors shouted out, "Your horse has returned and brought several horses home with him. What great luck!" The farmer replied, "Maybe so, maybe not."*
>
> *Later that week, the farmer's son was trying to break one of the horses and she threw him to the ground, breaking his leg. The neighbors cried, "Your son broke his leg, what terrible luck!" The farmer replied, "Maybe so, maybe not."*
>
> *A few weeks later, soldiers from the national army marched through town, recruiting all the boys for the army. They did not take the farmer's son because he had a broken leg. The neighbors shouted, "Your boy is spared, what tremendous luck!" To which the farmer replied, "Maybe so, maybe not. We'll see."*

It's easy to get caught up in pain or stress and begin thrashing, potentially making things worse, and it's tempting to spend precious time figuring out how the fire started when extinguishing it before it spreads is more important. How do you engage with pain or discomfort intentionally rather than succumb to its immediate intensity?

In this case, the first thing that needed to happen was for the CEO to swallow his ego and own the mistake. This wasn't the time for forensics, it was the time for responsible and meaningful action. He immediately got the leaders together and took responsibility. Later he told me that when he did that, you could almost hear tires screech to a halt. Everyone looked at him a little surprised and was then energized by him taking accountability. Everyone could focus their energy towards generating solutions to navigate the pain instead of the chaos of blame and finger-pointing.

So how did it end for this CEO and his executive team? In the end they were able to exhale. Reorient to what was important to salvage the deal, and take it across the finish line.

When you are faced with stress or pain, you can easily be overwhelmed by it. You focus on what it is doing to you, and you villainize it. Through a reactive misappraisal and a distorted narrative, you make yourself an object of the situation and your environment—an object that is tossed around and victimized by the situation. If this is you, stop it. Choose to be an agent that exercises the situation. An agent that takes on a deviant and masochistic mindset and meets the stress head-on, creating intentional pain to achieve long-term progress and elevate fitness to better prepare yourself and your team to navigate the inevitable turbulence that lies ahead. In the end, an object will see pain and obstacles as forces that cause pain and suffering. An agent sees pain and obstacles as opportunities for growth and invitations for action for which suffering need not be a requirement.

We've all failed. Hopefully you have. Some failures are bigger than others. Some feel like the world is coming to an end at the time, but in hindsight are only tiny bumps along the path. Some are critical events that shape who you are and enable you to handle difficult challenges far more gracefully than before.

Celebrate those failures. Over time, you will see or even feel the results of growth in your muscles. But it's easy to miss professional hypertrophic growth if you don't stop and look for it.

When I work with teams, I often ask the most senior leader in the room to share their biggest career failure—to talk intimately about the overwhelming emotions, the mistakes, and the specific details that were the hardest to deal with. Then I have them share the essential lessons learned from that experience and how it was critical in accelerating their growth. There is beauty hidden in the depths of despair that can transform a grimace to a grin.

Divorce, death, or bankruptcy can be nightmares that wake you up and teach you about yourself, better preparing you for what's next by building your skills, resilience, and confidence. Remember, it's all a simulation that can give you greater awareness, allowing you to become more intentional. You meet it, experience it, absorb the learning, and move on when you're ready.

The good thing is you don't have to wait for a nightmare to wake you up. If you embrace your role as a deviant agent that can masochistically maneuver the stress and pain in your environment, you embody the ultimate growth mindset. Remember, everything starts with your mindset.

THREE STEPS TO SIMULATION

The table is set. You are now prepared to embrace the key concepts of growth mindset: deviance, masochism, and simulation. Ideas and concepts without actions are useless. Now it's time to do some work. I'm going to take you through a few exercises to help you shape that meaningful masochism and become more aware of the pains in your environment. You can download the related worksheets at www.level52.ca/leadershipacademy.

There are two paths you can take when you experience leadership or organizational pain. You can take easy street and avoid it or take the masochistic approach and engage in the pain in pursuit of a vision that inspires you. Both paths have consequences that can lead to positive or negative outcomes. There are three steps you can take that will help you get closer to the path you want to be on.

To start, I want you to get a full understanding of the challenges you currently face. You need to get it all out. I mean all of it. List every single little irritation you complain about to your significant other or close friends. List each of the stressors that keep you up at night and write down the tremendous pains that make your heart ache. Use the table below as reference to list as many of each as you can. (Download and print the worksheet called CSP Inventory at www.level52.ca/leadershipacademy.

Complaints	Stressors	Pains
I'm frustrated that...	How do I...	I wish I would have...

Complaints are usually those little irritations in your environment that don't seem quite big enough to act on, like dishes being left on the counter in the lunchroom, a team member showing up late for your weekly meeting, low quality work by a team member, or maybe simply the way the person next to you hums while they work. These statements usually start out with, "I'm frustrated that…" Think about all your irritations, write them down, and let it all out.

Stressors are different from complaints as they have evolved beyond irritations into something bigger. These are the unsolved problems that keep you up at night. The mental churn that happens as you seek to fill a knowledge gap and solve an unanswered problem. Stressors could be, for example, pressure to meet deadlines, a consistent underperformer, people constantly coming to you to fix their problems, a collective lack of overall performance, unpredictable revenue, or inflated costs. These are significant things that occupy your thoughts as you lay your head down at night. These statements usually start with, "How do I…"

Then there are real, deep pains. The unexpected mistakes and nightmarish incidents that pull the rug out from underneath you. These heartbreaks are often met with regret, shame, and personal judgement. You got blindsided by a valued team member who chose to take another job and it leaves an enormous crater of competency. Maybe a key customer left to work with a competitor, leaving a gaping revenue rut. Perhaps you got pulled into a human resources visit because of accusations directed towards you for concerning behavior, or maybe you have to let some of your people go. These pains hurt to the core and challenge you deeply as a leader. These statements often start with, "I wish I would have…"

The reason for doing this exercise is to develop awareness of all of the little and big pains and obstacles in your environment. While not always the case, there is often a relationship to unaddressed complaints that compound into stressors. Ignored stressors that slip through the cracks can turn into shattering nightmares that jolt you awake into a new and present way of leading. Understanding your complaints, stressors, and pains is critical to your development as a leader. The quality of your list will determine the quality of your leadership exercise for the rest of this book, and really your career. All of the items in your inventory are potential opportunities for you to practice being a wonderfully deviant and purposeful masochist. However, sadly, you can't exercise all of them. Not at once.

ALL PAINS ARE NOT CREATED EQUAL

The irritating complaints, significant stressors, and paralyzing pains on your list can converge to form an overwhelming tsunami that creates significant distress and damage. The good news is that you can transform that intimidating force into actionable exercises in your leadership simulation. But first, you have to prioritize them.

To get clear about how you might prioritize your listed complaints, stressors and pains, let's dive deeper and plot them on the pain matrix below. (Download and print the worksheet called Pain Matrix at www.level52.ca/leadershipacademy).

The vertical axis of the matrix represents frequency. How frequently is the complaint, stressor, or pain occurring? Zero is rarely and a 10 is very frequently.

The horizontal axis represents the intensity of the pain, zero being a hardly noticeable irritation while a 10 is a life-changing pain that shakes the foundation of who you are.

Everyone experiences pain differently. Assess each of your pains and reflect on where they sit on the matrix for you, in this moment. It will likely change in a week or month, but chart your experience of right now. This exercise brings awareness to the different obstacles and pains in your environment and helps leaders see their challenges in a different light. Forcing yourself to arrange your pains according to frequency and intensity will prove to be a valuable monthly practice that will allow you to be intentional about what you engage in. It will reveal the difference between a real fire that needs to be dealt with and your addiction to being a firefighter. By identifying your pains and consciously separating them, they are transformed from a powerful tsunami of pain that's too much of a force to engage with into actionable obstacles that you can exercise to be better.

The pains that are in the upper right section of your matrix may likely require swift and immediate action, whereas something less frequent and intense (in the lower left section) can be put on hold while you deal with things that will make a significant and lasting impact.

Once you have plotted your pain matrix and have a greater understanding of the different intensities and risks, you can become intentional. Remember that you can't exercise everything at once. That's called over-training. If you ask a young pitcher to pitch his best fastball all game every game, you'll quickly end up with a depleted underhand beer league pitcher. Don't do that to yourself. What is important is to understand the implications if you don't exercise the challenges that matter most right now. You've got your list of complaints, stressors, and pains, and you have better awareness of their frequency and intensity after going through the pain matrix exercise. The next step in this process is to determine whether you engage in hypertrophy or allow atrophy.

Start by placing one of your pains or stressors in the middle column of the pain management table below. Let's say, for example, that you have a team member who is constantly underperforming. We will call this person Pat.

AVOIDANCE outcome	Reasons to AVOID	Pain/Stress
Pat continues to deliver poor work results. I work more to make up for and fix it. Eventually, I will fire Pat and hope the next person is better.	I do not have the time to keep giving Pat feedback and direction.	Pat is underperforming and sucking up so much of my already limited time.

Pain/Stress	Reasons to EXERCISE	EXERCISE Outcome
Pat is underperforming and sucking up so much of my already limited time.	Pat has desire, just not experience. Hiring a new person also takes a lot of time. I need to get better at my expectations, feedback, and direction.	Pat's performance improves and after a while, I can delegate more tasks which creates more time for strategic thinking.

Reasons to avoid this pain? Well, maybe you just don't have the time or energy to devote to giving Pat feedback again and again. Spending more time with Pat to make sure things are clear and supporting Pat takes way more than you can give. The outcomes will be that Pat continues to deliver poor results, you work more to make up for it, and eventually, maybe you'll just fire Pat, hoping that the next person will be better at their job.

What would the reasons to exercise this pain be?

Well, you have decided to take on this challenge and know that if you do it right, Pat will eventually get it. If you exercise the problem, you will get better at communicating clearly. You will get better at coaching and holding accountability. As a result, Pat will start performing, and over time, you will be able to delegate more. If you don't exercise the problem, it will likely only continue.

This tool is the starting point to understand the stories you tell yourself about the pain or stressors in your space. The narrative you tell yourself will dictate how you navigate those stressors, depending on what you are willing to take responsibility for. This can also help you become intentional about the choices you make. I constantly remind my executive clients that whenever you say yes to something, you say no to something else, and vice versa. This is why it's important to be extremely intentional about the complaints, stressors, and pains you choose to engage with and to know how they matter to delivering meaningful leadership in your business.

Sometimes, when we run our extended leadership training programs inside organizations, a client will ask us to help them explore getting another job elsewhere because their current situation is so bad.

Whenever this happens, my immediate response is the same.

"No, I won't. I won't do that to you and won't let you do it to yourself. Here's why: If you run away from all of the problems facing you right now and go get another job in another company, the same crap will follow you into your new shiny job once the honeymoon period burns off. Here's what we can spend our time on. Really identifying what's painful, identifying your responsibility in them, and developing a plan to exercise them differently so you can get a different result. It will take time and a lot of effort, but you'll become far better than if you avoid it and let it follow you into your next role."

This doesn't always convince them to stay, but most do. And when they put the work in, regardless if they stay or go, they become better because they've exercised the issue. Most, if not all of our problems, are a result of things we either have or haven't done.

As a friend's wise old uncle always says, "If everywhere you go smells like shit, you'd better check your underpants."

WHY EVEN FIGHT?

Time is precious, and people can be frustrating. Why would you choose to exercise and engage in some of these pains? And even if you start to exercise them, what will keep you going?

These are valid questions, and it comes back to the why of your leadership. Masochism isn't meaningful unless there is a purpose behind it. What is the vision you have for yourself and your team? And more importantly, why do you choose to lead? That simple question can make the difference between identifying the pains and giving up when it gets tough or continuing to make micro-progress that will eventually lead to a massive breakthrough.

There is an old story about candidates going through Navy SEAL training. This training is widely considered one of the hardest physical and mental tests a person could ever experience. As the story goes, each aspiring SEAL reaches a point where they are so taxed that they can't take the next step or get through the excruciating pain. It's at this exact moment that a savvy instructor gets down in the mud beside them and asks them one simple question. They whisper into their ear, "Why did you choose to be here?" This simple question connects the person with their intrinsic motivator—their desire to serve their country.

You need to ask yourself, "Why do I choose to lead?"

Get clear about your compelling reason to lead beyond the better compensation, fulfillment of ego, and authority or it just being the next logical step in your career. Really ask yourself why you are willing to go through the pain necessary to lead others. If you don't have an authentic reason, I'll tell you right now, you probably won't do the lifting to exercise your challenges. You'll take easy street and walk that path until a nightmare wakes you up.

CONCLUSION

Everything cascades from your mindset. The way you perceive pain affects how you engage with it. This will determine whether you react frantically in a state of distress or engage from a place of eustress. Stress, resistance, turbulence, whatever you label it, will either be a villain in your life or a vital asset to your growth. The difference between the two is how you look at it— your mindset.

Growth mindset means embracing hypertrophy and understanding that failure is a simulation that provides opportunity for improvement and growth. Transforming your business starts with hypertrophy—engaging in the pain and hard work required for lasting, resilient growth. By choosing positive deviance and purposeful masochism, you opt for hypertrophy and growth rather than atrophying on easy street.

The three exercises I took you through in this chapter will help you to identify and reframe the complaints, stressors, and pains in your environment. By investing time to take inventory of and prioritize these pains using the pain matrix, you will grow to understand them better. The pain management tool will help you to plan your approach to reframe your pain as part of your long-term leadership fitness plan.

This simple pain management approach will heighten your awareness and your ability to meet challenges head-on, differentiating you from other leaders and getting you further down the path to leading meaningfully.

THINGS TO REMEMBER

- A muscle subjected to stress and resistance adapts by growing.
- You are either in growth mode or protection mode, never both at the same time.
- There are two types of growth—sarcoplasmic and myofibrillar. One is fast and good for the ego, the other takes time and is sustainable.
- Deviance breeds innovation.

- You are either an object that is victim to your circumstances or an agent acting to influence your circumstances.
- Meaningful masochism is creating the necessary pain that will help you grow towards your inspired vision.
- Identify all your irritations, stressors, and pains, evaluate them, and identify what you should exercise.
- If you don't have a compelling purpose to lead, you'll likely not do the hard things. So, why do you choose to lead?

CREATE MEANING

Awareness: What are the things you complain the most about? What problems keep you up at night? What sharp pains are you dealing with?

Intention: What mindset do you want to engage with your complaints, stressors and pains?

Exercise: Get clear and intentional about what irritations, stressors and pains you will engage with and what you will avoid.

Reflection: Schedule time in your calendar to reflect on the mindset you find yourself approaching these items with. Are you expanding your ability to create better outcomes, or are you acquiescing, lamenting and waiting for a nightmare to wake you up?

4

VIRAL LEADERSHIP

One day, I was sitting on the couch eating a sandwich and watching some daytime talk show on the television. The guest on the show, a professional fashion consultant, was speaking passionately about what Hollywood's darlings chose to wear based on their body type. This was before smartphones, so I had nothing to distract me and was completely focused on listening to her go on and on about make-up, blouses, and then, Tom Cruise. She said, "Tom is a perfect example for you men out there. He's a shorter guy, and he's got a wider frame. Tom must wear vertical stripes. It helps him look taller and slimmer. As you can imagine, if he wore horizontal stripes, he'd look shorter and wider." I stopped eating my sandwich immediately and sat there with my mouth open as I absorbed this shocking news.

There I was, five foot seven and about 200 pounds, a classic short and stocky guy who spent most of his free time at the gym. I looked down, and to my horror, I was wearing a horizontal striped shirt. The last thing I needed was help looking shorter and wider. I was mortified. I ran down to my room in the basement, tearing off my shirt. I ripped open my closet and shrieked in agony at the sight of shirt after shirt bearing horizontal stripes. There they hung, quietly taunting me and my shrunken length and expanded width.

What did I do next? I picked up the phone and called a friend of mine, another short stocky soul who would benefit from this new and important information. It's been over 20 years, and to this day, I have never purchased or worn a horizontal striped shirt again. And neither has my friend.

Sometimes, an idea reaches you when you are in a susceptible state. Like a virus, it infects you and takes hold within you, ready and waiting for any opportunity to spread to other susceptible hosts around you. In this chapter, we will explore and exercise the concept of memetics as the next element in the Science Behind Success™ model, looking at how behavioral contagion and the viral life cycle impacts your culture and your ability to influence as a meaningful leader.

WHAT IS A MEME?

Richard Dawkins introduced the world to the concept of the 'meme' in his 1976 book *The Selfish Gene*. If genes are considered the building blocks of life, then memes are considered the building blocks of culture. A meme can be any piece of cultural information that is passed from person to person by imitation: anything and everything from people's habits, sounds, the way they tell stories, dance, or the clothes they wear.

A meme operates exactly like a virus. Despite the negative connotations of the term, for the purposes of this metaphor, a virus can be anything—not necessarily good or bad—that is capable of spreading. Once a virus finds a susceptible host and infects it, that host transmits the virus to another susceptible host. In the case of the horizontal stripes, I was a 20-year-old who wanted to attract a nice female partner, so I was very susceptible to any type of virus that would enhance that objective. I did my best to never let horizontal stripes hurt me or someone close to me again, and I passed on this wisdom to my friend, who passed it on to his friend…and on and on it goes. Viral contagion spreads quickly, and it has a significant impact on communities and cultures.

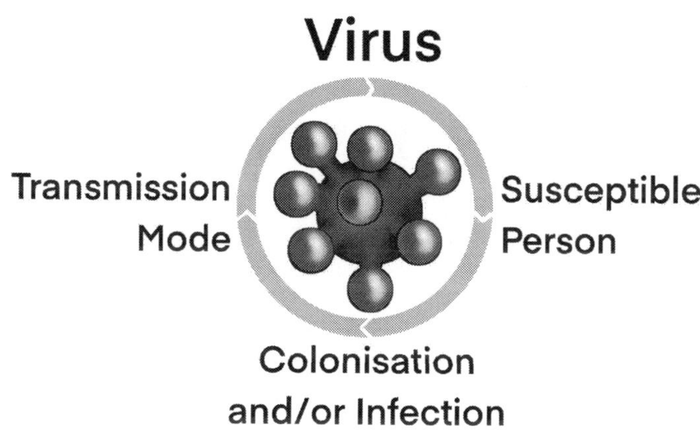

Viral contagion

There are both good and bad viruses inside organizations. As leaders, we must become aware of those viruses and identify which of them create critical momentum and which create cancerous downward spirals. Your business and your home are filled with very susceptible hosts, which means that the way you handle a virus is very important.

VIRUSES THAT SPREAD INSIDE YOUR BUSINESS

Earlier in my consulting career, while working inside a large multinational organization, I interviewed a new senior vice president to learn his business approach, leadership style, and 90-day strategy. I asked him several questions, but it was his answer to one question in particular that really piqued my interest. I asked him how he managed time and distractions. He replied with a half-grin and said, "Oh, that's no problem. No monkeys jump on my back. I close my office door to get my work done, and when I leave, I put my head down, look at my phone, and I walk fast." That was his method. I could envision this happening as he walked me through the steps, but what I couldn't ever have imagined was what impact this little thing would have on the entire organization.

I returned to the office about two months later and found that what used to be a place that gave off a sense of energy and socialization had been transformed into a quiet line of prison cells. Doors were shut and those walking around had their heads down over their devices, walking urgently towards their destinations. A virus had been spread.

You are surrounded by viral memes, and they are constantly trying to get your attention, colonize within you, and have you spread them to others. You are also constantly surrounded by susceptible hosts that are ready to absorb, host, and replicate the behaviors they think might make them successful. Think about a behavioral virus that was spread to you. You won't have to look far. The words you speak, the clothes you wear, and the way you work have all been adopted from someone else, most likely without you even being aware of it. Viruses are sneaky and powerful, and they are always seeking to maximize their fitness. In a world where Covid-19 has brought to our attention that viral pandemics can quickly take lives, we still need to accept that behavioral viruses are quickly killing the cultures inside businesses around the world.

Right now, do an informal viral analysis of your team or organization. What words do people use? What narratives are being told? What clothes do people wear?

Before starting Level 52, I was on the senior leadership team at the Coaches Training Institute, a learning and development firm based in the San Francisco Bay area. A few weeks into my time, and while getting up to speed on the company, I quickly noticed the way people responded when projects were being discussed in small group or team meetings. Most people would say the same thing: "I just don't have the bandwidth to get that done," or "We just don't have the bandwidth," or "We are currently having bandwidth issues." Bandwidth, bandwidth, bandwidth… everyone was blaming bandwidth. What does that even really mean!? I thought it was ridiculous. Clearly an excuse that had become en vogue and totally acceptable in that company as a way of avoiding workload. Here's the best part. A few months after I started working there, a friend of mine was asking me about something I was working on, and what did I say? "It's going ok, but I'm struggling with bandwidth." I didn't even notice until he pointed it out. Dammit. We are all susceptible.

Work-life balance is another prevalent virus. You hear leaders say it all the time. It's good for their people to respect it and own it so the workplace represents mental and physical wellbeing. It's generally accepted as the way things should be but often doesn't happen. Why?

Imagine the chain of viral contagion. A senior leader sends an email at 11:30 pm on a Thursday night. A different senior leader sends a text on Sunday morning. Another leader asks you to call him quickly on Saturday night as he's finishing a report and needs some quick info.

Imitation spreads much quicker than anything else, and it can be to you and your company's advantage or detriment. Have you ever heard the statement, "Your actions speak so loud I can't hear what you're saying?" This is the way memetics works. If work-life balance is a thing, make it a thing and model that thing, otherwise it won't be a thing, until it becomes the thing you didn't want.

Once you understand this, as a leader, you have to become more aware and intentional about the viruses you allow to infect you and the ones you intentionally spread.

THAT'S THE WAY WE DO IT HERE

Can someone get you to do something you'd never do? They probably can, and you probably wouldn't realize it.

A study of wild monkeys[8] led by Andrew Whiten from the University of St. Andrews is a great example of how powerful influence can be.

---

8 Lewis, T. (2013). 'Everybody's Doing It: Monkeys Eat What Others are Eating.' *Live Science*. [Online] Available: https://www.livescience.com/29048-vervet-monkeys-eat-like-locals.html.

His team of researchers studied four groups of wild vervet monkeys. The team gave each group a supply of corn with different colors: blue and pink. In two of the groups, the blue corn tasted bad, so the monkeys learned to eat only the pink corn. In the other two groups the situation was reversed. The pink corn tasted bad, so the monkeys chose the blue corn.

After almost half a year, the researchers switched the colors around, so what had tasted good now tasted bad, and vice-versa. However, the monkeys continued to eat only the color corn they had learned to eat, even though the taste was bad.

Baby monkeys that never had the chance to taste the good stuff only chose what their mothers ate, learning to eat the poor-tasting corn. They simply adopted their mothers' choice of corn. They were susceptible hosts that took on the virus of what food to eat, without exploring a better-tasting option. Even if the other food tasted better, they chose to mimic their mothers, because that's what successful vervet monkeys do, right?

This might seem like monkey business, but what about us? How many times have you made what was intuitively the wrong choice to impress others or fit into your new environment against your values and principles?

Leaders are a walking billboard that advertise to others how to be successful. Monkey to monkey, or human to human, you are constantly spreading behavioral viruses. Some that benefit and some that don't.

YOU ARE THE PROBLEM

Every week, I have leaders tell me about all of the things that are frustrating them—the reasons they are failing to meet expectations, either their own or from others. I get complaints about the little nagging things, and questions like:

"How do I get my employees to stop coming to me to fix their problems?"

First of all, understand that you are the problem.

Ok, take a breath. Go easy on me. Pick up the gloves off the ice (a hockey reference for the sports fans). I'm not going to get into a tussle with you, but I will tell you the truth. You are the center of all of your problems.

Take out your CSP inventory from the previous chapter and look at it. If you are like most leaders, most, if not all of the issues on your list will be either due to actions you didn't take or an action that didn't go right and you didn't go after it in a different way. Of course I'm simplifying it, but every problem essentially comes down to those two buckets.

Let's take a common leadership challenge.

Why *do* people continue to come to you to solve their problems?

We do an experiential exercise in our programs in which a leader is surrounded by three people. One person shares a personal story while, simultaneously, two others ask very simple questions like simple math or trivia. It is designed to be chaos, and the majority of leaders do the same thing: When asked to tell the details of the story back to the person, they can't. They spent so much time in the chaos focusing on answering the simple questions because it's what they knew, and it made them feel like they accomplished something in the moment.

Without very clear intention, our old habits from yesterday will continue to drive our behaviors today. These behaviors matter because they provide informal instructions to others. You are constantly training people how to work with you through the actions or lack of action you take.

When people come to you with their problems and you answer them, you train them not to think. So, they line up outside your office, waiting for you to save them. They wait for you to fix the problem, and you do it every time, opting to be the fearless knight in shining armor that rescues them from the fire-breathing dragon rather than give them the training and tools to take on the dragon themselves.

You might think I'm being dramatic, but admit it—if you are like most leaders, you do this all the time. It is a reward that fills you up with a little dopamine, and it feels good because you did something good. It takes you back to the good old days and that familiar metric of achievement. You helped someone by solving their problem. The problem is you are also creating a problem. If you recall in Chapter 1, leaders often get sucked back into the gravitational pull of their expertise and the seduction of their ego-reward system. You want to save people, to be the hero, the smartest person in the room. To flex your expertise and intelligence so you can pull a rabbit out of a hat and be recognized for being exceptional. You do this so when forced rankings come (if your company still uses this) you don't get the dreaded 'valued contributor label' because that would mean you are simply average—a cog in the wheel instead of the singular thrust of the entire mechanism.

I think you get my point. Your environment shaped you this way. Your behavior is the product of many years of expertise and reward and feedback mechanisms…AND it will hold you back as a leader.

The sooner you understand that you are the center of all the problems you complain about, the sooner you can examine the viruses you've been spreading and have a fighter's chance to resolve them.

THE 'BUSY' VIRUS

Just like the blind spots you can't see as you back into parking structures, there are viruses you become so comfortable with that they seem normal and don't appear to be a problem.

I once worked with a client who was a leader in the technology industry. He held a strong vision to disrupt his industry through the way they used technology. He was passionate and driven to change his business but unfortunately was infected with a common virus.

One day he asked me, "How can I lead effectively when I've got so much work to do?"

I'm referring, of course, to the virus of 'busy'—a strong and deadly soul-sucking pandemic that masks itself as a shiny badge people unconsciously celebrate with passive-aggressive pride.

'Busy' is an easy and lazy answer to everything. It's probably what you'll answer if I ask you how you are doing. Or if I ask you why you are late or what stopped you from getting something done. If I ask you why you didn't have that important conversation. If you are like most people, the answer will be the same: I was too busy.

The biggest risk to the long-term success of your company is not competition, and it's not market conditions. It's one simple thing: busy.

Think about all of the things that you don't have time for:

- You don't have time to properly clarify expectations on what people should deliver—the result is disappointment at their performance and more work on your plate as you fix their work.
- You don't have time to coach or develop your people—the result is a lack of improvement and the continuation of bad habits and underperformance.
- You don't have time to have an offsite with your key leaders or your team—the result is a lack of alignment, trust, cohesion. You know, all of those things that are luxuries and non-essential. I hope you sense my sarcasm.

Be very cautious of the busy disease. I'm not perfect and can be just as susceptible to it as you are. It is a vicious and persistent virus that requires frequent treatments to keep it at bay.

'Busy' has a gravitational pull that takes you out of intentional action and into a slumber of mindless routine. You stop making time for process improvement because you're busy.

You don't make time for post-mortems or lookbacks that make things better because you're busy. You don't take the time to leverage the intelligence in your company and collaborate to solve your problems because you're busy. You race from meeting to meeting unprepared, and you stop focusing on getting better for tomorrow because you are in demand right now and it's hard enough to keep pace, let alone get better. 'Busy' results in shortsightedness which, when unmanaged, can lead to a degenerative condition that negatively impacts the way you lead and can quickly spread throughout the organization. Are you showing your team that being busy is more important than anything else?

Being busy is strangely comfortable. You allow yourself to get consumed by never-ending meetings, pandering to instant demands instead of considering what is really most important. Being busy can create the illusion that you are effective. If you do not pause and ask yourself what is most important, then everything becomes important, and when everything is important, nothing is important. This is when time becomes a scarce resource, and you'll often choose the path of least resistance, which means instead of coaching and course-correcting your people, you do the work yourself and stay busy. This further perpetuates the scarcity of time and the busy virus, and the cycle continues. It's part of the inescapable prison you create for yourself and spread to others.

So how can you break out of the prison of busy? How do you stop yourself from constantly fixing people's problems and fighting fires as they break out? What is the difference between making success happen yourself and creating the conditions for success? You can download a worksheet on how to fight the busy virus from our website (www.level52.ca/leadershipacademy), but I'll also give you a short example here.

New leaders often tell me: I feel bad when I delegate. If this is you, ask yourself, what do you feel bad about? What assumptions do you have about delegating? How might you reframe the negative story about delegating into something that is an opportunity to develop people?

If you have difficulty managing your choices, try using a framework like the Eisenhower Matrix[9] or the Getting Things Done Method to help you get on track and get some time back and stop transmitting the busy virus.[10]

---

9 'The Eisenhower Matrix: Introduction and 3-minute Video Tutorial.' *Eisenhower*. www.eisenhower.me/eisenhower-matrix/.

10 'David Allen's GTD Methodology.' *Getting Things Done*. 22 June 2019.

Time is a precious currency. When you become a master of your time and create the foundation to trade that currency intentionally, you will reduce the incredible burden that comes with trying to keep pace and will instead spend some of it investing in your future. That is a virus worth spreading to others.

MAKING YOUR VALUES A VIRUS

It's easy (and irresponsible) to pick on those viruses that quickly and negatively spread throughout your organization, and that isn't fair. Because when done well, leaders can also take the concept of memes and viruses and use it as an intentional tool to influence the mindsets and behaviors they want to see in their teams. Yes, you can use an intentional virus to your advantage.

A question many leaders struggle with when asked is, "What are your organizational values?"

I once asked a senior leader of an organization I was consulting for this question. She paused for quite a while, furrowed her brow, named one, paused again, named another, and then winced as she said, "I can't remember the rest."

Organizations love to display fancy words that they claim as their core values and guiding principles. You see these values on the website's 'About us' page, and you see them at the desk at reception. Some of the most common are:

Integrity, honesty, trust, accountability, commitment to customers, passion, fun…

These are only a few examples of what companies SAY are important to them. Yet when I ask leaders to tell me about their values, they often struggle to name them. I'll keep poking this bear and say that actually,

---

www.gettingthingsdone.com/.

these values aren't CORE in any way the company operates. In fact, they don't seem to be valued at all.

Let's start with integrity: Think about the daily decisions that are made inside your organization that aren't made with integrity. Honesty: How often are lies told inside the walls of your company? Trust: How much do you trust the people you work with? What tools and strategies are used to help people develop trust in your company? I've worked with several companies that have trust on the wall as a core value but struggle with it mightily. Accountability: Are the leaders in your organization really able to create and hold accountability with their reports and peers? In my experience, not very well. Commitment to customers: How is your company committed to its customers? As a customer myself, I've had many interactions where I definitely did not experience this promised commitment. Passion: Is this really a core value in your organization or something you wish people had? Fun: Hmmm. Well, if fun is a core value then it's hidden quite well in most organizations. I often go into a business and see people who can't wait to race out the door to get away from the place where their heart tends to hurt the most, the place where they aren't recognized for their contributions, where they are constantly asked to do more with less time and less resources, and on and on.

If this sounds familiar to you, why do you have these words on the wall? I'm here to tell you not to have core values unless you are one of the rare organizations that actually embodies their values. Pretty values on a wall mean nothing if you don't use them as a tool to spread powerful viruses, using them as key building blocks to create the foundation for meaningful performance.

If you are not going to use values as a viral device inside your business, it's better to just lose them. If you don't throw them away, people will roll their eyes and shake their heads at the lack of integrity in the business. It's true. Throw them away. Save yourself from having to dust off the facade, and just focus on plugging away in your valueless environment.

Or, use your newfound knowledge of viral transmission and become a lean, mean meme machine. Make the values in your company into something real.

You can start by identifying what your organization's values mean to you. Then explore how you actually embody them in the organization and get intentional in how you walk the talk. As you now know, over time your behavior will spread through the business through imitation. Creating clarity for yourself is the first stop. Once you've done this, you will create clarity for others as well. They'll clearly see what the values mean and will be able to envision how they should embody them in their work. In Chapter 6, I'll introduce you to some tools that will help you create and communicate clarity and create a critical feedback mechanism that churns out positive viruses.

Make your values important viruses. If you don't, you might as well save the ink and the space on the wall and the website and get rid of them completely.

MISSED OPPORTUNITIES

Remember, a virus is not always a bad thing and can have a very positive influence in your organization. Rebranded, the word can represent opportunities, or in this case, missed opportunities.

How often do opportunities to spread powerful viruses slip past you? Viruses that could potentially create momentum, inspiration, and recognition, leading to greater performance. There is no shortage of opportunities around you. You just have to spend the time looking, develop the ability to spot them, and when they arrive, jump on them like a fierce jungle cat.

One of my clients, a fast-paced and highly reactive global business, once faced significant turbulence. They brought a group of key people together to discuss some important changes in the business and asked me to help them facilitate the meeting. Clients often ask me to sit in on these meetings, either to facilitate or simply observe and give them unbiased feedback on their communication, behaviors, and impact. In the boardroom with me were a handful of senior leaders who were leading a virtual meeting that included about 50 of the next-level leaders. The most senior leader spoke to the group about the daunting challenge in front of them, presenting slides to explain the changes and create context. While explaining the significant challenge that specifically impacted one region, he spoke to the obvious, "As you can see, Dave's area has the biggest challenge of us all. For those of you out there who can't see him in this room right now, Dave is looking at these numbers and is under the table here cowering and shaking at what's in front of him and his team."

I looked over at Dave to see a stoic and slightly unimpressed look on his face.

The meeting continued. New targets were set, and the team was sent off to begin planning to address the pivot in strategy.

After the meeting, I debriefed with the senior leader and asked him what his intention was when he referred to Dave. And I get it—he was trying to make light of what was a big challenge. But the reality is that it was a missed opportunity.

I shared the reaction I observed Dave having and asked the leader what he really wanted to infect his group with. Remember, you are always spreading viruses, either ones that create momentum or ones that create downward spirals.

The leader said he wanted to spread viruses around **rising to the challenge, taking initiative...**etc.

Okay, so what if he had approached it differently? He could have said, for example:

"As you all can see from this slide, Dave and his team have the biggest challenge out of all of us. Now, most leaders would be cowering and shaking under the table, but Dave and his team have been doing a lot of hard work, they are ready for this, and if anyone can do it, they can, and so can the rest of you."

The leader agreed instantly that he had missed the opportunity to create critical momentum and quickly put together a plan of action to make it right. He decided to own the missed opportunity on the next team call, speak to what he wished he would have said, reinforce the belief he had in Dave's team, and point people to where he really wanted them to focus.

As a leader, you are never short on opportunities to create empowering viruses that instill the behaviors that lead to success. You are never short on spotting potential in others that remind them and reinforce why they can do things.

Meaningful leadership means doing the little things that make the biggest difference in your team's fulfillment and performance. The tiniest things can greatly influence your team's ability to do great work. These are the subtle yet significant viruses that will either create or kill resourcefulness.

BRILLIANT AND PLEASANT VIRUSES

Do your small actions have an impact on how others create? Do you have the power to conjure up a spell that transforms the intelligent into the idiotic? Can you evoke brilliance with a small but significant action? In the late 1990s, two Dutch professors sought the answers to this question and did a study with university students where they had them answer several Trivial Pursuit questions.[11] The students had the same range of academic standing and were asked the exact same questions, however, what was different were the conversations they had before the quiz started.

One half of the students were asked to think about and write down what it would be like to be a professor. The other half were asked to sit and think about soccer hooligans and the fanatical actions that led to violence and riots. The result? The students who thought about professors got 55.6% of the quiz correct, whereas the other group got 42.6%. It's not

---

11 Dijksterhuis, A., and Van Knippenberg, A. (1998). 'The relation between perception and behavior, or how to win a game of Trivial Pursuit.' *Journal of Personality and Social Psychology*, 74(4), 865–877. [Online] Available: https://psycnet.apa.org/record/1998-01060-003.

that the professor group was smarter. They were simply put in a smarter frame of mind.

Everything cascades from your mindset and the mindsets of the people on your team. Do you create viruses that evoke a smart frame of mind or do you rile up hooligans to run your asylum?

Wait. If there's a smart virus…is there also an angry virus?

If you haven't been to New York—believe me, it's pretty busy. Sidewalks are packed shoulder to shoulder. People dart rapidly from one place to the next, quickly navigating the busy crowds to get where they need to be. Nobody in New York likes to waste time. Could you influence more patient behaviors in people who are so used to a rapid pace?

In 1996, John Bargh, a professor of psychology at NYU, sought to answer this question as he delivered a priming study in which he gave all the students in the experiment one of two scrambled-sentence tests.[12]

The first test's sentence consisted of words like aggressively, bold, rude, bother, disturb, intrude, and infringe. The second had words like respect, considerate, appreciate, patiently, yield, polite, and courteous.

After students completed the short test (which took less than five minutes), they were individually instructed to walk down the hall and go talk to the person running the experiment to hear what would happen next. However, it was staged so that the person they needed to speak to was engaged in conversation with someone else. How long would the students wait for the conversation to end before interrupting to complete their task?

The results were interesting.

Those who had worked on the word puzzle with aggressive words

---

12 Bargh, J.A., Chen, M., and Burrows, L. (1996). 'Automaticity of Social Behavior: Direct Effects of Trait Construct and Stereotype Activation on Action'. *Journal of Personality and Social Psychology,* 71(2):230-244 [Online] Available: https://www.psychologytoday.com/files/attachments/5089/barghchenburrows1996.pdf.

interrupted the conversation after an average of five minutes, while those who had worked on the puzzle with more pleasant words never interrupted, and the experiment was stopped after 10 minutes.

Focusing on little things like priming your day and that of the people on your team is next-level intentionality, but I want it to be the bar you set. How do you start meetings? What is plastered on the wall? What music is playing? Remember, everything is a virus. How do you prime the people on your team to be creative and collaborative instead of complaining and self-pitying? Whatever you do, consider it an advertisement that promotes or prevents what is acceptable in your organization.

Here's the thing about advertising. Conscious of it or not, you are a walking billboard. You are a meme machine and are always advertising to others how to be successful in your organization. Everything you do has the potential to spread, and it impacts not only the behaviors people take on but also what they say and do. Unfortunately, you don't have the ability to see your blind spots and likely aren't aware of some of the viruses you spread. This is why 360s have become an integral part of our starting point in executive and leader development. When done well, a 360 can really help you identify the viruses you spread for better or worse. Advertising is important when you consider the susceptible host, or the internal or external customers that are constantly buying from you. Yes, buying from you. Even if you are in accounting, you are constantly selling something: ideas, processes, everything. The question is, do people buy what you sell them? It all depends on how you've built your brand.

WHAT'S IN A BRAND

Think of a place where you like to eat, things that you like to buy, and services that you choose to spend your money on. Why do you do it? Why do you go to the same restaurants over and over? Why do you fly with a certain airline carrier or engage with your preferred services?

You likely buy your shoes from a preferred supplier and book your flight with an airline you've had good experiences with. Just as importantly, you stay away from places that have underdelivered or created poor experiences. You do this because you have developed associations based on your experiences with these brands.

The same thing applies to you and your leadership. People engage or avoid you based on their 'customer' experiences, whether good or bad, or with a big or small sample size. This impacts how they choose to engage with you and if they 'buy' what you are selling.

It's important that you understand the building blocks of a brand so you can not only analyze what your current and unintentional brand might be but can get intentional and shape the brand you want moving forward. The four building blocks of a brand I want you to get familiar with are: Feel, Think, Say, and Do. To help you with this you can download some leader brand worksheets at www.level52.ca/leadershipacademy.

Feel

What do people feel when your name is brought up? When they see you in the hall? When they imagine you on their drive into work? When I get people to describe their best and worst leaders (see Chapter 1), you can almost see the feelings ooze out—either gratitude and celebration or resentment and frustration.

What do you want people to feel when they describe you? Inspired and challenged, or deflated and distracted? They will feel something, so what do you want it to be?

Think

Just like people feel things based on how they experience you, they also think things based on their experiences. For example, if I am working for a leader who supports and encourages me, I might feel really empowered by them. If I feel empowered by them, I might think that they really value me and the contributions I make inside the company.

Understanding this, the next logical question to ask yourself is, "What do you want them thinking about you based on your ability to lead?" Are they thinking, "This leader has my back," or, "This leader believes that I can reach further than I have been," or, "This leader is willing to block and tackle to help me be successful?"

Based on how you engage with people, what do you think they think when they think about you?

Say

Regardless of how much businesses advertise, it's often word of mouth from satisfied customers that leads new clients their way.

People describe the relationships you have with them in the way they speak and the stories they tell about you in casual conversation. Whether at the water cooler, happy hour, or at a business picnic, people will tell stories. The associations they hold will inform the narrative that takes shape. Is it a story of complaining and victimization or is it a story and words of fulfillment and excitement? If I feel empowered by my leader and believe they value me and my contributions, what would I say to others about this leader? Probably a story that expresses how much I enjoy working for them and can't imagine working for someone else.

What do you want the people who work with you to say to others about you? What do they actually say about you? Are they working for you, with you or against you?

Do

The final, most important and measurable building block of your leader brand comes down to action. What are the actions people take as a result of how they feel, think, and talk about you?

If I feel empowered and think that I'm valued, and I tell others how much I love working for you, I'll probably come to work prepared, exercise creativity, and do my best to consistently demonstrate my value.

What about the opposite situation? If I feel like our interactions have been transactional and you've been dismissive and judgemental, I might feel stupid and incompetent when I'm around you. If this is the case, I probably think that you wish you had someone else working with you and it's only a matter of time before I get fired. I likely tell others how disrespected I feel and how I dread Monday mornings. The actions I take are to hide my mistakes from you, and I walk the other way when I hear you coming.

What are the actions you want people to take as a result of experiencing you as a leader? Maybe they'll avoid you if it's a fear-based relationship. If you're highly transactional and you tend to fly off the handle or disproportionately discipline people when they make mistakes, they'll avoid you like the plague.

People will engage with you the same way they do with a consumer brand. Now that you know the building blocks of a brand and have analyzed what your current brand is, you stand at the precipice of transforming your old and unconscious brand into your new and intentional brand.

This is the beginning of a new era in your leadership as you plant your flag, wear your colors with pride, and embrace extreme intentionality through spreading memes that matter.

THINK Based on recent feedback, what do people think about you and your leadership?	**FEEL** Based on recent feedback, how do you make people feel based on your style of leadership?
SAY Based on recent feedback, what do people say to others about you and your leadership?	**DO** Based on recent feedback, what are the actions people take based on their experience with you?

WHY A BRAND?

There is a big problem with being a good leader, part of the time.

Foundations are important when you are building anything, so when I onboard a new client for a coaching engagement, I begin with a foundation session. The foundation session is important for us to get to know each other, crystalize the focus areas of the coaching, and to develop a road map. It also helps me to get a good understanding of how the leader views their world. During one such foundation session with a new client, he was sharing all of his perspectives on the progression of his career and the current challenges that were facing him. He was transparent, not hiding anything and just laying it all out on the table. He said, "I just sort of figure out my leadership approach as I go—no real specific method. But you know what? I'm really stressed out from trying to do everything and be everything to everyone. And at times I don't know where I should focus."

The impact of this person figuring things out as he went led to inconsistency in his approach, and a team that lacked direction, ambition, and that was often frustrated.

Studies show that given the choice between working with a leader who is sometimes good and sometimes bad or a leader who's consistently bad to work with, people would choose the consistently bad one. Why?

When there is a consistent force in their environment, people can develop strategies to deal with it. It's inconsistency that makes it difficult to work with people (or live with them)—when you don't know how they're going to respond or what they're going to do at any given time. I'm guessing you don't want inconsistency from the people you work with, and you also don't want people to experience you as an inconsistent leader. So, define your brand and the consistent impact you want to have on others.

When I did a 360 on this leader, it came out that some of his peers and reports felt frustrated. They questioned his ability to make decisions, and the chatter around the water cooler wasn't overly positive. People tended to avoid this leader, as they felt the interactions caused more confusion than they provided clarity. His brand needed to change. The challenge is that it takes a long time to build a strong brand and a short time to damage it, so getting clear about your impact and committing to the practice of consistency is important.

When you are clear about the brand you want to express in your environment, you can step into a place of **extreme intentionality.** This is the standard I hold for meaningful leaders. Extreme intentionality becomes the compass for how you respond to others and the lens that informs how you navigate the challenges you will undoubtedly face. Instead of being shocked by a 360-feedback process, your unintentional billboard and the viruses that spew from it, you and I are going to co-isolate together and build you a new brand. It's going to be authentic, aspirational, and unapologetic.

I'd be remiss if I didn't mention that some people really dislike the word 'brand'. Taken the wrong way, it can seem self-promoting, fluffy, or manipulative. I get that you can see it that way, and there may be some who use it that way, but regardless, we all know you have a brand. Why not be intentional and create a clear and authentic brand to guide you in building consistent impact and value for others? If you absolutely need to call it something other than brand, then you're welcome to consider it your reputation, but in this book, I will unapologetically call it your leader brand. Okay, now that we are on the same page, let's get started crafting yours.

AUTHENTIC, ASPIRATIONAL, AND UNAPOLOGETIC

What does it mean to be authentic? When it comes to leadership, I believe authenticity is a genuine and true expression of who you are, who you want to be, and the impact you want to have on your world. The key word is 'genuine'.

This is something that young and experienced leaders often struggle with because they've spent much of their career trying to be the leader or manager they thought they should be instead of grounding themselves in a place that's real for them. It's the difference between getting clear and intentional about who you want to be as a leader and unconsciously absorbing leader viruses and mimicking those around you. It comes back to the question, why do you choose to lead? If your answer inspires you, it's likely great grounds for an authentic foundation. What do you value most? Get clear and understand that, as it's the fabric of who you are and an important foundation for how you lead.

If authenticity is about the fabric of who you are, the aspirational element is about who you are becoming—the qualities you want to deliver and the legacy you want to leave behind.

Start with the qualities you want to bring as a leader. It can be helpful to ask yourself what the qualities you've appreciated and admired in other leaders are. What is it about those qualities that had an impact on you? It is useful to be able to visualize and connect with the behaviors and qualities demonstrated by impactful leaders so you can take the ones that feel right to you. For example, one of my favorite leaders had a way of being present with others, and she was also bold and a straight shooter. Those are qualities I've taken from her that are a part of my aspirational component.

Create a list of no more than five qualities you want in your brand. If you haven't already, to help you with this exercise, download the fillable pdf at www.level52.ca/leadershipacademy.

Once you have your list of qualities, ask yourself what impact you'd have if you expressed those qualities consistently over the rest of your career. Will your legacy be stories people use to demonstrate powerful leadership or stories about what not to do? At your retirement party, will people be in tears as they celebrate you and the way you shaped their careers and supported them when times were tough, or will they be celebrating the fact that they don't have to see you again? What will you be known for? What impact did you create? How did you enable others? Give yourself permission to envision the powerful legacy you created as a result of intentional leadership, and aspire to embody the qualities that will get you there.

This isn't the end though. To create this powerful legacy, what do you need to take a stand for?

The unapologetic aspect of your brand is the piece that can be most challenging for many leaders. It's also the one that can take you from being a good noticeable leader to a game changer. One that creates innovation, changes culture, and stands out as a disrupter. It means making something else more important than being liked.

Gasp! But what if I'm not liked?

Let me flip that on you. What if you're the most liked person in your company but you never really do much to boost performance? You don't push or challenge people. You don't give them the real feedback they need to be better.

In my career as a young leader, I didn't really take a stand for anything. If there was something I took a stand for, I guess, it was two things. Doing most of the work myself, and…being liked. I really didn't want to disappoint people. So, I avoided discomfort, didn't give feedback, and with deep resentment and frustration created a world where my mantra was a victimized tune of 'I'll just do it myself then.' Don't be me.

What will you take a stand for?

Do you take a stand for performance and give fast and furious feedback? Do you take a stand for creativity and innovation, constantly pushing boundaries of what's possible? Maybe you take a stand for safety, ensuring everyone goes home safely to their families. Whatever it is, just please, please, get intentional and take a stand for something. Be unapologetic about what matters to you.

Having clarity about what you stand for can really help you navigate the choices you make as a leader when the pressure is on, and it can also have a cost benefit. Take, for example, this scenario that was very real for many leaders: During the beginning of 2020, the Covid-19 crisis rocked the entire world. These were unprecedented times for any leader. People had to stay at home, businesses came to a complete halt, and it was a time of endless questions and elusive answers.

Imagine you are the leader of a small-medium sized business during this crisis. You have 20 to 30 employees, and everything comes to an abrupt halt. You rely on the day-to-day business activities to keep the lights on and aren't fully confident that your receivables are going to get paid. You don't have much of a runway, maybe three months at most. What do you do? You have to look into the whites of people's eyes and take the lead. What do you stand for?

If you worry about being liked in this situation, you are screwed. You'll probably avoid it—hum and haw until the situation has gotten really bad for everyone, forcing you to let them go because it's the only option left. Maybe you take a stand and direct that everyone takes a 50% pay cut for six months so nobody has to be let go. Maybe you take a stand for transparency and collaboration and give people information about the challenge so you can come up with a solution collectively. Maybe you take a 'cash is king' stance and quickly let people go, hoping they'll come back when things become more certain.

If you are very clear about the unapologetic aspect of your brand and are consistent with it, people might not like your choice, but they will probably respect it. The point is to take a stand for something and invest the time and energy into understanding how that might play out in everything from your ideal state, your day-to-day environment, as well as times of crises.

Note of caution. I want you to get clear and be unapologetic about something. But be aware that the people around you might wonder what the hell just happened if all of a sudden you start showing up wildly different at work (I'm not talking about 'post-Burning Man' different). I've seen leaders get really clear about what they stood for only to go passionately rogue inside their businesses in a very unproductive way. I'm telling you this because there are important steps you need to take that create context for others about the unapologetic part of your brand. Don't blindside them—create a heads-up to prepare them for how they can expect you to show up. More on this in the next chapter.

To be unapologetic is to not acknowledge or express regret about decisions or actions that are in line with your brand. This doesn't mean that decisions necessarily become less difficult, but they can become clearer for you and others, helping you keep the implicit and explicit promises you make to others. Every day you make promises that you probably aren't even aware of. You make promises to your kids, to your significant other, and to the people around you. Some promises you keep, and some go unfulfilled.

YOUR BRAND PROMISE

A brand promise is a statement that captures the authentic, aspirational, and unapologetic elements of your brand in a brief statement. We use the term 'brand promise' instead of a personal purpose statement or a mission statement, as clients seem to find this less overwhelming and more practical. This is the epicenter of your personal meme generator so you can deliver meaningful leadership.

Your brand promise focuses on the intentional brand you want to infuse your work culture with. Remember, every interaction in the day is an opportunity to demonstrate the behaviors and associations you want to create in your organization. When you use a brand promise to help create the trajectory of your day, you step into the verb of your leadership—the practice of it, not falling into the misconception that leadership is a destination and understanding that it truly is a daily intentional practice. It takes a long time to build a powerful brand and a short time to lose it. When you get clear about the impact you want to create and the brand you want to express, you can begin the path of building your brand or rebranding your leadership to operate with greater precision and consistency.

You are always promising something, often unintentionally in the way you show up. What do you promise? Geico promises 15% savings if you give them 15 minutes of your time. What do you promise to give people when they interact with you? Is it judging and criticizing them for making mistakes? Taking credit for their hard work? Stealing their evenings and weekends so you can have yours? Distraction and disconnection? Or is it something that creates resonance?

Beyond just being descriptive or aspirational, your brand promise should be something you do to provide more value to those around you. This is your opportunity to practice and communicate a consistent approach to your leadership. Think about what matters to those around you. What do your customers want and need that you are positioned to deliver? A brand promise is a tool to orient your leadership approach and a way for your team to hold you accountable to the standard you want to model in your environment.

Some examples of intentional brand promise statements are:

- Present, passionate, and pushing you to be better.
- Obliterate complacency and elevate you to rise to the challenge.
- A trusted ally in success, failure, and growth.
- Shining a powerful light through the fog to help you see better.
- Cutting through BS so you can focus on what matters most.

You get to make your brand statement whatever you want it to be. But make it real for you. Make it authentic, aspirational, and unapologetic.

Here's the tough thing. It takes a long time to build a powerful brand and a short time to lose it. It's a long-term, daily practice of getting clear and delivering consistency. Practice extreme intentionality around the impact and value you want to create for others, and over time, your brand will blossom as you spread the viruses you want and stop those you don't want.

CONCLUSION

We are all aware that real viruses can take lives, but there are behavioral viruses that are rapidly killing cultures. The viruses and memes in your organization can be good or bad, and when used intentionally, can be a small but incredibly significant tool in your leadership. The key is for you to get clear about the types of viruses you want around.

First, you have to accept that you are a walking billboard, advertising and spreading viruses and memes through your everyday behaviors. It's not enough to just have your values on the wall—words don't mean anything. To be a consistent and effective producer of memes that matter and viruses that lead to victory, you need to pause and get clear about what you advertise to others. You need to determine what you stand for, what you aspire to be, and what legacy you hope to leave behind once your career is over.

Once you understand the building blocks of your brand, you can express them in a single, clear statement—a promise of what you seek to deliver to those around you. This central tool will help you spot little opportunities that can have a big impact inside your organization.

Through intentionality, planning, and the commitment to engineer the behaviors you want, you can leverage each and every opportunity to model your values and build your desired legacy. You are always advertising to others how to be successful, so make sure you are advertising the right things.

Extreme intentionality is a big job. It's definitely not for everyone. I did tell you it's simple. It's just not easy. Are you still up for it?

THINGS TO REMEMBER

- Memes are the building blocks of culture and spread just like a virus.
- Memes and viruses can be good or bad.
- Be conscious of the viruses you spread. They either create critical momentum towards what matters or create cancerous downward spirals.
- How do you prime the people on your team or in your organization?
- You are a walking billboard that advertises to others how to be successful. What are you advertising?
- People will feel, think, say, and do things based on the associations they develop by experiencing you.
- Whether you like it or not, you've got a brand. Get clear about your authentic, unapologetic, and aspirational brand.

CREATE MEANING

Awareness: What has my unintentional brand been? What associations have others created based on their experience of me?

Intention: Create your brand. How do I want people to experience me moving forward? What are the authentic, aspirational, and unapologetic qualities I can demonstrate that will create meaning and impact?

Exercise: Identify the viruses you want to stop and start spreading to deliver a powerful brand inside your organization.

Reflection: Schedule time in your calendar to reflect on the impact of your brand promise.

5

ENGINEERING YOUR ENVIRONMENT

In the sport of bobsled, you spend a lot of time training in the off-season to prepare for a five-second push. Seeking to perfectly orchestrate that moment of timing, explosive power, and speed to accelerate the sled as fast as possible. Countless hours are spent every day in the weight room and on the sprint track in an attempt to shave a 100th of a second off your start time, because one 100th of a second advantage in your start time translates to three 100ths at the bottom of the track—in theory. Hundredths of seconds at the start determines the difference between playing with a lead or catching up.

As a much smaller pilot than the others in the world cup circuit, the way I trained was important. Already an average high performance athlete, I needed every bit of time I could find.

What created the right environment for me was taking an uncommon approach.

I was used to a strict training program—knowing what I was doing for each training cycle with wonderfully graphed periodization and analysis. But what got the best results from me was something completely different. It came through the arrival of a surprising and unconventional figure. His name was Andrzej (we called him Andy) Kupczyk.

Born in Poland in 1948, Andrzej had been a world-class middle-distance runner, finishing seventh at the 1972 Olympics in the 800-meter event. A multi-national champion in Poland, he was known for his expertise in developing athletes. Although he came from Eastern Europe, his coaching style was not the science-driven, ironfisted rule you'd expect. It was completely the opposite. Our training was more like Sylvester Stallone's in Rocky IV. In the early phase of our training cycle, we weren't in the weight room or on the sprint track like other athletes. Instead, you'd find us bounding on grassy fields into flocks of Canadian geese while the rain poured down on us. Or we'd be standing ankle deep in the water, throwing large rocks into the river. Despite our complaints about his approach, Andrzej remained committed to an uncommon environment. He'd have us sing songs during excruciating abdominal workouts while the lactic acid burned our cores. He taught us basic Polish and always referenced our exercises by their Polish names. It felt crazy, and it shouldn't have worked. But it did. He created an environment that engaged us and made us work harder.

After working with Andy for a while, I clocked the second fastest 30 meter out of everyone at a national testing camp. Andy's methods were unconventional and unorganized, but they worked for me. He was eventually let go despite the results he created. His methods were too outside of the box—too different from the blueprint national team coaches were supposed to use. After he left, my testing results were never the same.

How did Andy do it? He found a way to create an environment that got the most out of his athletes. He made each person important. Most of our training group was made up of mid-range, high performance athletes that he was able to creatively and intuitively get the most out of. He focused less on the common and acceptable blueprint and created the conditions for success for each individual athlete, even if it broke some rules.

Your organization has rules and blueprints that guide it to be successful. As a leader, you also have formal and informal rules that guide you. Together, all these rules and conventions form a blueprint that becomes your guiding DNA.

I'm here to tell you that this DNA is less important than you think.

Next, we will explore the traps that come with the infatuation with blueprints and metaphorical DNA and will look at what you should focus on instead. By the end of this chapter, you'll have a deep understanding of the third element of the Science Behind Success™ model, what culture is, and why it matters to you and your business. All of this insight will come through the lens of epigenetics as we use science to understand how you can influence the expression of your organizational DNA and engineer your culture before it engineers you.

DNA DESPAIR

If only we had smarter people, more resources, or more time. Imagine the things we could achieve. Have you ever heard leaders say something similar to this? Have you ever let these words come out of your mouth?

I have. I am guilty of succumbing to DNA despair. Pointing fingers and blaming reasons like not having the right people to fix the problems in the business, enough money, or enough time to get to where I want to go. There are leaders who fall victim to DNA despair and complain about things like this, and then there are leaders who understand that more money, more smarts, and more time does not guarantee anything.

In the mid-1800s, Samuel Pierpont Langley, a professor at the famed Smithsonian, was commissioned by the U.S. Department of War to develop a heavier-than-air piloted airplane. He had a head start and the equivalent of a genetic advantage—access to the smartest people, money, and resources. Everything you think you need to be successful. The 'DNA' was all lined up for Langley and his impenetrable Smithsonian team to succeed. But, as we all know, the Wright brothers beat him to it.

How did two brothers with no venture capitalists, angel investors, or savvy financiers behind them beat Langley and the well-funded minds of the Smithsonian? They had no substantial formal education and little financial resources—everything we hold as important ingredients to achieve high performance in business. Yet the Wright brothers didn't allow themselves to get sucked into the black hole of DNA despair—that false 'truth' that you are only a product of pedigree and victim to your genetic limitations. Instead of focusing on all the things they didn't have, they focused on what they did have. They possessed an unwavering belief that they could do it. They had vision and passion that shaped a powerful mindset that led to powerful actions.

Remember, the way you see things determines the way you engage with it. The Wright brothers harnessed something more important than a blueprint or list of prerequisites. They harnessed culture. They embodied the concept of epigenetics—the science that explains, as Peter Drucker said, why culture eats strategy for breakfast. The Wright brothers peered into the eyes of their metaphorical DNA and laughed in the face of the genetic joke.

THE GENETIC JOKE

Remember science class in high school? It's likely we all learned the same things from the same Bunsen burners, bullfrogs, and textbooks, based on the same beliefs at the time.

We learned that genetics are the building blocks of everything, the causal agent in life and the composition of traits and characteristics programmed at the moment of conception. We were led to believe the primacy of DNA, genetic determinism, and the fatalistic narrative that we are controlled by our genes as if in a movie that was already written. Basically, you either won the genetic lottery or were dealt the genetic equivalent of recycled toilet paper. It all comes down to luck, buddy! You're either fortunate or you're f…unfortunate. Based on this information from our trusted educators we learned to celebrate, accept, or lament our predetermined paths. Depending on the luck derived from your gene pool, you identify your lane and you stay in it, free from the burdens of responsibility or agency.

You, like many others, have fallen into the strong and inescapable gravitational force of the black hole that is the great genetic joke. The joke that leads you to believe that only people with certain experience have the right DNA to succeed. The joke that leads you to believe that only people with the right competencies can drive your business forward. The joke that leads you to believe that your strategic plan is a magic bullet for proven process.

Just like success doesn't simply come down to the divine gift of genetics, there is so much more to high performance than your DNA. Does it help to have the genes of a thoroughbred? Of course it does. Does it automatically translate to success? It sure doesn't, yet many leaders and business people buy into the genetic joke.

DNA and genes are the equivalent of 'truths', imperatives and strategies that you believe will make you or break you. These are the rules you've made up and the excuses you hold as to how and why you and your business are successful. Unexamined, they can lead to disappointment, disaster, and a tear-stained diary titled "What should have been."

DNA is no more than a blueprint. What matters most is how that blueprint is brought to life. Genetic determinism is no different from strategic determinism inside your business. It's foolish to think that your strategy and blueprint is your destiny. Your genes are made up of a hereditary blend that is determined at the moment of conception, and your strategy is nothing more than a strand of ideas and concepts based on yesterday's intelligence. What you do with that DNA and how you activate it to be successful is far more important.

A blueprint is simply a plan. A collection of the rules and DNA that tell you how something 'should be'. If I walked into a room of 100 people and gave each of them a blueprint to build my dream home, how many of them would actually capture the excitement of my vision? They'd do their best to put this home together based on the specs, and then they'd be forced to make some quick decisions at certain periods of the process that aren't clear in the blueprint. Crown molding? Stainless steel appliances, oh yeah—wall color. What about landscaping? Some of the difficult decisions weren't specified in the blueprint, so decisions had to be made. In the end, based on how different people perceived the same blueprint, there will be homes that look quite different.

Your genes act in a similar fashion. Your DNA and genes are simply instructions that form a blueprint. You can't live in a blueprint. It's simply a concept that provides instructions. In the case of a building, you need to transform that blueprint into something spectacular. It's what happens with the blueprint during the process of interpretation of the instructions and the communication of the plan that determines how grand that expression is. It all comes down to epigenetics.

EPI WHAT?

Epigenetics literally means 'above' genetics. The term was first coined by development biologist and Cambridge professor Conrad H. Waddington in 1942, and its meaning has since evolved significantly. Initially, epigenetics was simply about genes and their hereditary role. Later it became about the process of an egg becoming a fully-fledged organism, and then it moved on to focus on hereditary traits that involve no alteration to your DNA sequence through things like methylation and signal transduction. A whole book could be devoted to trying to explain the intricacies of the epigenetic process alone, but instead I'll take my shot to do it simply and effectively, and then translate it to why it really matters to you and your business.

Your DNA is the blueprint or code that carries the instructions that tell your genes what to do. Methyl groups in the DNA bind to genes, giving them very strict orders to express themselves or not. The methyl groups attach to cells differently, which helps them understand whether or not they are a skin cell or a muscle cell.

Another key player in the process of epigenetics is histone. These are proteins that act like little spools the DNA twists around. The looser the DNA is wound around the histone group, the more the gene is expressed, and the tighter it's wound, the less it's expressed. The methyl groups act like a switch that turns the genes on or off, and the histones act like a knob that turns the volume up or down.[13]

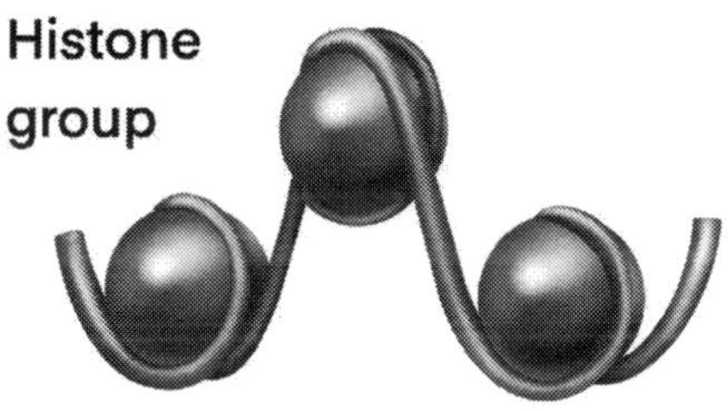

DNA wound around histones

To put it simply, your genome (DNA blueprint) does the work, and the epigenome (interpretation + communication) tells it what to do, leading to the ultimate expression of that blueprint. The wrong inputs (like instructions and expectations) can lead to methyl groups binding to the wrong place, which can cause mistakes, abnormal growth, and ultimately disease.

The first time I was exposed to these concepts, I started thinking about how my poor communication as a leader influenced poor results. My being so tightly wound was influencing how creative and expressive the people on my team were. Had I made my 'blueprint' as a leader more important than everything else?

Understand this. No blueprint works on its own. No blueprint will take you and your business to the promised land. It's how you work the blueprint that matters most, and as a leader, it's understanding the inputs

13 'Epigenetics.' SciShow on Youtube: https://www.youtube.com/watch?v=kp1bZEUgqVI.

that affect expression and the quality of communication that enables the greater expression of the organizational genome (collection of talent).

PERCEPTIONS, PUPAS, AND BUTTERFLIES

If you take three stem cells with the exact same DNA and you put them into three different solutions, one stem cell will grow bone, one will grow muscle, and one will grow fat. It's the same DNA and the same stem cell—why and how would each of them grow into something different? The answer lies in the environment. The different solutions influence the activity of the methyl groups and the expression of the DNA.

This is not just something that happens in a Petri dish—it happens inside of you too. Once we understand that we ourselves are walking Petri dishes,[14] we understand that it is our perception and environment that influence the release of the neurochemicals that inform how we express ourselves into the world. Your perceptions create inputs that affect your personal expression. You've got the same DNA every day, but there are situations where you show up differently.

For example, let's imagine you get no sleep one night. You show up the next day, dragging yourself from one meeting to the next, cursing life, and you don't know how you're going to get through the day. What's happened? You've gotten no sleep. You've just had a new baby and that baby was up crying all night. If you're like me, you're crying just as hard as the baby because you don't know what to do.

Let's compare that to a similar but slightly different situation. Imagine you get no sleep one night. You walk to work with a skip in your step the next day. You're high-fiving strangers, you've got a theme song in your head, and you've got a literal glow. Life is amazing. What's happened? Well, you just met someone you've fallen in love with. You've been awake all night having, you know, stimulating conversation and maybe even making lists of all the things you want to do together, exploring each other's dreams.

---

14 Lipton, B.H. (2016). *The Biology of Belief 10th Anniversary Edition: Unleashing the Power of Consciousness, Matter & Miracles.* Hay House Inc.

That kind of stuff. Your body is filled with oxytocin, dopamine, life-affirming neurochemicals that have you jumping into your world, ready to go and on fire. You get no sleep in both situations, but you're showing up much differently.

Everything you do is an input into your environment. It starts with the environment inside of your head. What are the perceptions, the emotions that fill your body? The culture and solution inside of you that alter your expression? This impacts what you express into your environment at home, within your team, and your organization.

Genetically, there's no difference between a caterpillar cocoon and a butterfly, but they are expressed remarkably differently into the world. We've all been in situations where we were slow and sloppy like a caterpillar or shut off from the world in isolation (or a cylinder of excellence, as experts like to call them) like a cocoon. But we've also experienced greater expression of our capabilities like a butterfly. It comes down to how you interpret and perceive your environment and the way that alters your expression and those around you.

CULTURE AND EXPRESSION

What are the truths you tell yourself that get in the way of your success? When acquiring talent and developing your organizational strategy, it's very easy to get completely focused on the metaphorical DNA of your company—to allow blind 'truths' to convince you what you need to be, have, and do to be successful. And just like if someone gave you a blueprint to your dream home and said, "Enjoy your dream home," you are left standing there holding a piece of paper that you can't live in. Your organizational strategy is nothing more than a concept—a plan. How that plan is transformed into reality will be determined by the things that actually happen in your business: how the strategy is interpreted, communicated, and modeled.

How many of you have experienced this: You hire a top talent—someone socially dynamic and expressive. They come in, they dive into the culture, and six months later, you're wondering why they're not the same person you hired. What is it that's made them slow and sloppy? Why aren't they performing based on what their resume promised? They certainly aren't the person who showed up in their interview!? This was someone that was supposed to come in and be a game changer. What happened?

Paper champions don't equate to success, not in sport, and not in business. You can buy the best talent or have the best strategic plan on paper, but if you have a toxic culture, poor communication, or allow complacency, all of those paper lions will quickly deteriorate into the pulp of lambs. CVs and strategic plans are like aspirational DNA strands just hoping to show up as the best version of the blueprint. How is it possible that someone with the perfect pedigree can't perform, or the proven strategic process turns into nothing but the Pied Piper's dream?

The inverse is also true. As the Wright brothers proved, it's also possible to get the right result even when you have the 'wrong' blueprint. A company that is not enslaved by the trap of competency tunnels knows to look beyond the simplicity of the resume when searching for a candidate, considering instead how the right DNA could be expressed in the right conditions.

I was once co-presenting with a leader from LinkedIn at the Association for Talent Development (ATD) conference, the world's largest talent development conference hosted in North America. It brings together tens of thousands of trainers, consultants, human resources experts, and business leaders seeking to learn the latest and greatest methods to enhance their teams. While we were preparing our presentation, my co-presenter shared with me a story of career progression inside his company. An employee who had worked on their finance team for several years had expressed her desire to get into new product development. Her mentor, who was well connected, indicated that a position had opened up to lead a product development team. When the employee found this out, her first response was, "I can't do that! I have no experience in product development." Her mentor pushed her and told her the qualities she possessed that would be a valuable addition to the team. Despite not having the DNA for the role, she decided to apply. My co-presenter told me that this employee would never have gotten the interview if she had been an external candidate. But in this case, she got an interview and delivered. She got the job despite not having the resumé DNA most organizations would require. How did she do? As the story goes, after a year, she had led the team in developing the most profitable LinkedIn product that year.

Someone's competence will stand out when it's in the right context. It's about creating and enabling people to create their conditions for success.

APPLYING EPIGENETICS TO YOUR LEADERSHIP

The stage has been set. Now that you have a basic understanding of epigenetics and why it matters, you can start focusing on how to get the greatest expression out of yourself, your team, and your organization. We are about to get really instructional.

The remainder of this chapter consists of two parts. Part one is focused on getting the most out of your direct environment: your direct reports and colleagues. The second part is focused on the larger organizational environment. I'm going to take you through a series of exercises and tools that will help you take ownership of and maximize the expression of the different cultures in your organization. Take your time. Identify how you can apply it to your world and remember, make the time you are spending meaningful.

PART ONE: APPLYING EPIGENETICS TO YOUR RELATIONSHIPS

Epigenetics teaches us how important it is to be accountable for your environment—your own environment, as well as that of your team and your organization. As a leader, you are responsible for three layers of culture. The first is your own culture. That skin-covered Petri dish you walk around in every day. No one else can own it but you. Start to investigate what it is that helps you be more like the greater expression of your DNA and what it is that gets you into caterpillar territory.

Three layers of culture

The second layer, which is what we will be focusing on here, is the team and relational culture. Every relationship and team have a unique culture. There are tiny, different signals that impact each microculture, and your ability to diagnose and deliver the right inputs will increase the likelihood that your relationships and team are at their best.

The third and final layer of culture is the organizational culture. The mosaic of mindsets, narratives, behaviors, and artifacts that bundle together to make yours. We'll discuss this layer later in this chapter.

You are responsible for each of these layers, so proceed with caution. As Dr. Bruce Lipton says, "Once you become aware that you are responsible for everything, you are responsible for everything."[15]

Everything is a Petri dish filled with (mostly) invisible inputs that affect your expression. Your own Petri dish is the biochemistry inside your skin. The inputs into the Petri dish of your relationships and team consist of a bundle of communication, assumptions, and the memes and behavioral viruses being spread. The inputs into your organizational Petri dish are

15 Lipton, B.H. (2016). *The Biology of Belief 10th Anniversary Edition: Unleashing the Power of Consciousness, Matter & Miracles.* Hay House Inc.

the combination and consistency (or not) of the narratives and viruses spread inside your company.

YOUR PERSONAL CULTURE

YOU ARE WHAT YOU EAT

How can you take ownership of your Petri dish and engineer your personal culture? What inputs affect your expression as a leader? What makes you slow and sloppy, what shuts you off from the world? What are the inputs that produce the most confident and best expressed version of you?

What you eat and drink has an impact on how you show up and express yourself. Fast food in a professional athlete's body will get sub-par expression. Poor fuel in a race car will negatively impact performance. Garbage in, garbage out. What you watch on TV, listen to, and read shapes your perspective. Garbage in, garbage out. What you spend your time doing, whether it's sitting or exercising, has an impact. Practicing mindfulness… you can go on and analyze all of your personal inputs. It all comes down to a simplified understanding of garbage in, garbage out. This simple principle applies to your leadership and organization and the inputs that affect the expression of your environment.

In Chapter 4 we looked at some of the viruses you need to inoculate yourself against. Now dive deeper into really examining the environment you expose yourself to. Do you generally surround yourself with people who push and challenge you to be better? Or do they conspire to keep you small, allowing you to blame external factors for a lack of results and villainize others who stand in the way of success? Whether true or not, it can be effective to examine the statement that you are the average of the five people you spend the most time with. Think about who those people are. What values do they embody? Are they negative or positive people? What stories do they tell? What missions are they on? Do they spread viruses that create momentum or cancerous downward spirals?

We will look at more individual strategies and how you can approach your own culture in the last chapter of this book. For now, we will focus on team and relational culture.

TEAM AND RELATIONAL CULTURE

What makes a meaningful and high performing relationship? Most people will give me the same answer or variations of the same answer: Common goals or objectives, mutual respect, trust, and great communication. If you and I work together, we've got our own culture. If you throw one more person into the team, the culture changes. Every person added into our team changes the culture slightly or significantly, depending on the combination of people on the team. Your job is to do what you can to enhance the quality of each team culture.

I'm going to take you through this step-by-step so you can understand what we call the critical inputs that affect the expression of your relationship culture. When you embrace these and make them important, the different cultures you own will change for the better. We are going to get hot and heavy into inputs, skills, and tools that will transform your leadership and your culture. But these skills won't do a thing if you don't have the right context behind them.

So, let's get clear about your role as a relational input. There is a part of your role that in itself will change the way you work with people and will change the way people work with you. This is often the missing input in a relationship that prevents growth and satisfaction. We will soon dive into role clarity as an important part of creating the conditions for success, but before that, I am going to set the stage by taking you into a space filled with grunting voices and clanking metal plates. We are observing a high performance gym, but we aren't watching the chiseled athletes as they activate force against resistance. We are observing a critical input in the success of an athlete, and that is the spotter. That person who stands behind them while they lift. The role of the spotter is essential but so easily missed if you aren't looking for it.

What does a bad spotter do? A bad spotter is a lazy, distracted one who has good intentions but negatively impacts your growth. Most of the time, bad spotters are looking at themselves in the mirror, admiring what other people are doing, or more worried about their own advancement. Bad spotters will see when you are struggling and grab that bar and rack it for you. They'll smack you on the shoulder and get the satisfaction of a little bicep workout themselves. Too many leaders lead and support their people this way. You grab that problem from your people and lift it for them, stunting their growth.

Now what about a great spotter? They will watch you struggle. They will champion you and remind you why you can do it, even when you doubt yourself. They will resist the temptation to grab that bar, even though it would make things easier, and will instead ask you to give more. They might put their fingers on the bar to give you a sense of security while you search to find the power inside of yourself to push it up and reach levels you never thought you could. The only time a great spotter grabs that bar and lifts it is when you are at risk.

Great leaders spot like this. They champion their people to go through the discomfort so they can find the strength and resourcefulness to push things over the finish line themselves.

What does this look like in your business world? Great spotters in the business world demonstrate a few critical inputs that transform the expression of their people. They listen, ask high-impact questions, create clarity, and design intentional relationships. As positive deviants and meaningful masochists, they let their teammates struggle to find the solution. They lift their own weights. If you are like most leaders, you might be thinking, but what if they are choosing the wrong thing and put the business at risk? This is where your self-management comes in. If something presents a great risk to the company, you need to lift the metaphorical bar. Don't put your business at risk, but also discern whether or not a little failure can actually be the pain that facilitates the next leap for your team.

Being a great spotter is a critical input that will transform relationships and results. Be one. Get one.

Let's look at the smaller but significant inputs that allow you to be a transformational spotter in your business.

LISTENING

Get ready to get sick of me, but I'll say it again: Garbage in, garbage out. The first critical input is one so simple that if it's not pointed out, you'll likely bypass it for a bigger cultural weapon. This critical input is listening.

I don't need to teach you how to listen. You know how to listen, but what you likely don't know is where to focus your attention, which is a fundamental part of the skill. When used right, listening is a fundamental, keystone skill that leads to many more wonderful leadership skills.

In the book *Co-Active Coaching*[16], the founders of the Coaches Training Institute (CTI), Henry and Karen Kimsey-House explain the three levels of listening and how the skill of listening can be cultivated. They call it the 1,2,3's, and we've adapted them into the C,D,E's: competitive, discovery, and empathetic listening.

COMPETITIVE LISTENING

Competitive listening is listening primarily to yourself or your own thoughts or agenda. You're likely thinking what to say next in the conversation and only half-hearing what the other person is saying. You listen to prove a point, one-up the other person or compete for voice space.

As an expert, you are taught to listen to solve the issue and close gaps on problems quickly. It's important to be able to do that, but it is a very transactional method that will hold you back as a leader.

When you listen with a competitive focus, the attention is on you, what's in your mind, and what you think about what the other person is saying. You listen to your own thoughts, opinions, judgements, and feelings. When you listen with an unconscious and competitive focus,

16 Kimsey-House and Kimsey-House. (2018) *Co-Active Coaching: Changing Business, Transforming Lives.* Nicholas Brealey Pub.

you are pretty much unaware of the person speaking and are simply filtering what is being said through your own interpretations and experiences, completely oblivious of your impact on the person speaking. You listen to them talk and will often interrupt with advice or a story from your experience.

At times, you may want to be good at competitive listening, but the problem is that most leaders operate from a competitive focus consistently. Competitive listening is great when you need to solve a problem, but as a leader, it's your job to help people solve their own problems. So stop relying on competitive listening and move it on up to focus on discovery.

DISCOVERY LISTENING

When I was on my first date with the woman who is now my wife, we were engaged in such a deep discussion that the lights in the restaurant started flickering. The server came up to tell us that we were the only ones left in the building other than the staff and they were waiting for us to leave so they could go home. We were completely oblivious to anything else going on around us because we were so present and curious with one another. Nothing else mattered. This is an example of extreme discovery listening. You are *intensely focused* on what the other person is saying. Nothing is distracting you.

Instead of focusing on your own thoughts, ideas, and advice, you hold a sharp focus on the other person. You are deeply curious and are listening for specific words and expressions to ask more questions about to discover more about them. When you are present and listening from a true place of discovery, you can often recall many of the details of what the other person said. This is the space where you can generate growth, exploration, and robust discussion as you get really curious.

The input provided by discovery listening is twofold. First, it has the person speaking to you feel genuinely valued because they have your undistracted attention. Second, you can ask great questions (more on this shortly) because you are receiving better data rather than creating your own interference as when listening with a competitive focus.

EMPATHETIC LISTENING

What would a blackbelt ninja version of listening be? You'd see things other people easily miss. Like a sixth sense, empathetic listening is also directed towards the other person, but it has a wider focus to hear things beyond just the words they're saying. You start to notice other things—body language, the inflections and tone of their voice, their pauses and hesitations. When you listen with an empathetic focus, you can bring in your intuition. Not in a crystal ball kind of way, but you might say things like, "Hey Jayson, when you talk about your work this week, I notice there isn't a lot of enthusiasm around your actions. What can I help with?"

The art of listening takes time to develop, but it can, and should, be practiced daily. It is especially useful in your one-on-one meetings, when negotiating or persuading others. It builds trust and understanding. In a customer service role, listening and understanding is imperative to building and maintaining relationships.

Listening is a critical keystone input that will enable you to do so much more, but it starts here. If nothing else, learn to self-manage your heavy reliance on competitive listening and shift the focus to discovery listening. When people feel listened to, they feel like you care about them, which causes a release of dopamine and oxytocin. As an empathetic listener, you will become a more resonant leader and will have much better data to work with. Both of these are essential inputs that affect the expression of your culture.

CURIOSITY KILLED THE CAT

Curiosity may have killed the cat, but it will act as lifeblood to your leadership and the meaningful culture you are creating. You've probably lost most of it. That's just what happens when you develop a strong expertise.

You naturally accrue more answers than questions, and the unintended result is that you lose your curiosity and seek to appraise rather than explore. But the pursuit of greater understanding relies on curiosity being a foundational part of your leadership. It's an essential input that comes from discovery listening and then forming high-impact questions.

What are high-impact questions?

- They are extremely curious, often about one of the last words a person said.
- They are open-ended, meaning they can't be answered with a yes or no and often start with the word 'what'.
- They are short and simple. Long-winded questions rarely create impact.

Let's take a common situation and apply discovery listening, curiosity, and high-impact questions.

Someone from your team comes to you with a problem they are challenged with. You self-manage your expertise and get curious about it. Remember, your job is to have the person exercise their thought process, not to steal the learning opportunity away from them.

You ask: What's challenging about it for you?

They respond with something like: It wasn't what I was expecting from them and I'm not sure what to do.

You ask: What are you sure of?

They respond with a long pause and then say: I don't know. *(Which is a really easy way to get lazy about something and it generally is a covert operation designed to get you to solve their problem for you.)*

You ask: You've been here a while and understand the business. I know you know something about this, so what DO you know?

They respond with: I know that I can do a better job of communicating beforehand so this doesn't happen again.

You get curious and ask: What does better communication look like?

You can then continue to drill deeper and clarify the core issue, helping them do the lifting to solve their own problems.

You see the difference? Normally, you'd probably give them a prescription, tell them what to do to get them out of your office, and then move on to the next task. Listening and asking high-impact questions takes a little bit of time, but after a while, you'll notice that your people are suddenly capable of so much more. They'll start coming to you with more complex issues that actually require thought partnership rather than the little ones that steal time away from you and growth away from them.

People hire me to be their executive coach mostly to listen and ask the simple questions other people won't and don't. Start to do this for your people and you will elevate awareness to different heights, and that deeper understanding will create a better expression of their talent.

You can download a full list of high-impact questions from our resources page at www.level52.ca/leadershipacademy.

Now that you're equipped with the foundational arsenal of inputs, I'm going to up your game and teach you an advanced skill that will bring a new level of clarity to you and your team. It's called bookending.

CLARITY AND THE ART OF BOOKENDING

Did you know that more than half of the birds in New Zealand cannot fly?[17] One of the reasons is that even before humans arrived, over 1000 years ago, there were no land mammals that would prey on the birds. So, with no predators sniffing them out, trying to take them down, there are

---

17 Goldrick, C. (2017). 'The weird, flightless birds of New Zealand.' *Australian Geographic*, 25 October. [Online] Available: https://www.australiangeographic.com.au/topics/wildlife/2017/10/the-weird-flightless-birds-of-new-zealand/

birds like the kiwi and some others that didn't have to work as hard to stay safe. They didn't have to go through the extra effort of flying in order to survive. But does this type of evolution serve the overall fitness of the species? Removing the predators from any environment might seem like a good thing, but it is exactly what will lead to a lack of fitness, put you into a domesticated slumber, and paint a target on your side.

One of my previous clients was a senior leader in the energy sector who was specifically brought into an organization to act as an ignitor. He had a large task in front of him. The company in question used to hold the majority of the market share in the country, but due to external environmental factors, results were quickly diminishing and the team needed a flat-out disruption. About two months after this senior leader was brought into the organization, we were in a meeting discussing the situation and he told his team that they needed to take more ownership of their areas. He was frustrated about the lack of action the team had taken since he started there. Nothing had changed, and things just weren't happening. Nobody was taking ownership. This is where I asked him a simple, high-impact question: "What is ownership?"

He paused to think for a moment and said, "Well, it's taking responsibility for your area of the business."

"What does taking responsibility for your area of the business mean?"

I could sense him getting frustrated, as to him, the answer was obvious. But this is exactly the problem—assuming that things are received on the other end, or that something is, or should be obvious. The catalyst required for any transformation begins with clarity.

We all use shorthand, vague, and nebulous expressions or concepts when we communicate, and yet expect other people to know exactly what we mean. I often sit back and observe meetings or observe leaders and the way they communicate, and it's remarkable how regularly this happens. You use these vague concepts in your communication all the time, not just in business but in your personal life as well, in your relationships and your marriage. This is what creates those unnecessary micro-pains that never get addressed, growing and causing bigger issues and frustrations that lead to fractures in your relationship.

If you don't really drill down into what you mean when you communicate, you'll likely leave a meeting thinking that everyone's on the same page, only to be really frustrated or disappointed when you meet up again and discover how divergent the trajectories of your isolated expectations and the actual results are. Without pursuing 100% clarity, the likelihood is that everyone will approach things differently.

I see it all the time from leaders. Below are some of the common vague terms I encounter all the time, and I'm sure that you can add many more to this list:

> "I need to see more from you."
>
> "We need to up our game."
>
> "This needs to be better."
>
> "I need to see A+ quality on this."
>
> "I need you to take the lead on this."

What do any of these vague phrases really mean?

If you want better behaviors, expressed values, and a higher quality of work inside your organization, it's your job to ensure that everyone is looking at the same detailed picture. Create clear bookends for your people, not only so that they understand expectations at a greater level but also to provide clear standards everyone can use as an informal form of evaluation.

Bookending involves painting a very clear picture of your expectations by describing what it is (the ideal) and what it isn't. Start with the best possible result and describe it in detail. What it would look like and feel like. In the case of ownership, clarify the ultimate expression of ownership.

Explain what you'll see people doing, what you'll hear them saying in meetings, how they will behave. Go into as much detail as possible about what the ideal expression of ownership would look like.

Once you've done the work to really clarify the ideal state, it's just as important to clarify the other end. What ownership is *not*. How will you know with certainty that leaders aren't taking ownership? Get really clear about the behaviors, what people do and say, that will clearly indicate they aren't taking ownership. All of this clarity is important for you to understand so that you can communicate it effectively. If you can't communicate your expectations clearly and you create inconsistent and ineffective feedback mechanisms, your team will likely assume they're doing the right thing.

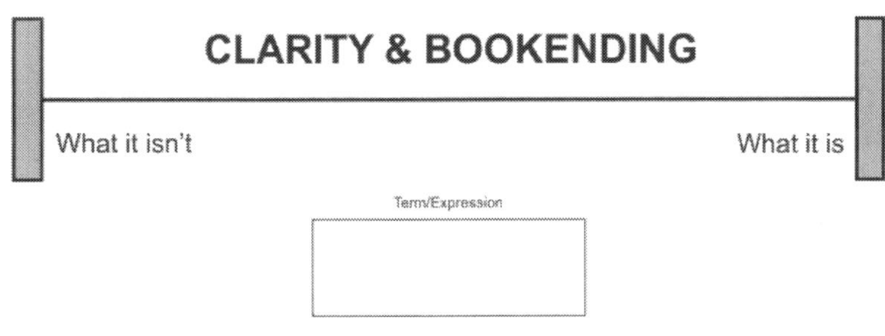

Clarity and bookending

Meaningful performance happens on the edge of struggle and support. As a leader, it's your job to hold both as equally important. Clarity and proactive feedback are essential metaphorical predators that keep your organization on its toes. Losing the ability to fly might feel good when you don't have to put in as much effort, but that quickly changes when someone else, like a competitor, can take advantage of it.

As a leader, you need to provide clarity so that your people know not only which direction to fly in, but how hard you need them to flap those wings, when to land, and when they can take a break in the nest. It comes down to you owning that clarity and then giving them the feedback that lets them know where they stand between the bookends.

THE F BOMB AS AN ESSENTIAL INPUT

The 'F' word needs to be used by leaders at work way more than it is now. It can be uncomfortable, seen as unacceptable, and is often misused and misinterpreted. But it can be a critical kick in the butt that inspires your people to pivot, course correct, and dig deeper. Yes people, we're talking about feedback.

One of the biggest complaints I get from all levels within organizations is that their leaders rarely give feedback, and when they do, it isn't very good. Organizations spend millions of dollars globally training people on how to give effective feedback. There are great models out there, and people still don't do it. Why?

Most leaders hold a certain perspective about feedback. It's hard. It's uncomfortable. It might upset someone, and you don't want to be disliked. This perspective prevents you from making it a priority. You rationalize not giving feedback and say to yourself that it really isn't that big of a deal, so you sweep the issue under the rug. Because, you know, it will get better over time on its own, right? The result is you generally wait for huge problems to occur before doing something about it, and then it ends up being an exercise, like trying to turn the Titanic. It won't turn on time, and the outcome won't be a good one. Remember, complaints transform into stressors that can become painful nightmares.

Here's what's even more messed up about all of this. You are constantly giving feedback through your inaction, behaviors, and lack of acknowledgement. NOT giving feedback is a form of feedback that unconsciously shapes the habits and behaviors of those on your team. You are training people how to respond to you by both the actions you take and don't take and by the words you say and don't say. It's a power bundle of assumed feedback that generally creates issues at some point.

Let's make this really simple: Intentional feedback is everything when it comes to developing your people and being another essential cultural input, yet most leaders do a terrible job at it and it's something people on your team yearn for. Here's what I tell all leaders. Not giving intentional feedback is one of the most selfish things a leader can do. That's right. Not giving intentional feedback is one of the most selfish things a leader can do. Sit with that. It's selfish because either you aren't confirming and celebrating the great work your team is doing, or you aren't course correcting them, letting them walk into the next room with metaphorical spinach in their teeth. So, confess! If this was you, then you used to be a selfish and lazy leader. Today this all changes.

The first step to great feedback is understanding that you are a custodian for your people's development, and that the feedback comes from a place of service to them. In fact, we often refer to it as feedforward, because when done well, it elevates the ability of the people on your team, moving them further down the line. It takes some work upfront, but it will serve you greatly down the line in being a critical feedback mechanism for the development of your people.

Intentional feedback starts with your mindset. Remember, you are a spotter. You spot the hell out of people to reach greater heights. You see the benefits of pain and stress and the way it facilitates growth. You listen with a discovery and empathetic focus and you ask high-impact questions. And you give great feedback. Think back to the unapologetic and aspirational parts of your authentic leadership brand. How does your brand express feedback? How does it give life to your legacy?

Peter Jensen, a famous sport psychologist who has worked with numerous Olympic medalists, speaks about how people can get really lazy in how they communicate what they actually want people to do. Those of you who have ever played baseball or have seen children learn how to play have all seen a kid standing up at bat, swing, and not make contact with the ball, over and over again. What do you tend to say to these kids? "Keep your eye on the ball." Okay. So, what do they do? This kid bends down. Their eyes get bigger, and they bring their head down more towards their waist level. They actually have no idea what you're trying to say. You get frustrated because, of course, it makes sense to you, but they have no idea what the heck you actually mean by keep your eye on the ball. Whereas if you just got a ball, and with a marker, you wrote big letters on each side of the ball, and you said to them, "When I throw this ball, I want you to be able to tell me what letter was on that ball," that helps them focus their attention on exactly what you want them to achieve. This is a much clearer way of describing what you want them to achieve rather than being lazy and using a hackneyed expression.

Being specific is really important when you are trying to redirect or course correct behavior or the quality of work. When things aren't where you expect or need, it's time to redirect and get them on the right path. ASAP. Don't wait until annual reviews or your one-on-one meeting. Do it now and do it quickly.

It's important to prepare feedback before you deliver it, so that it's concise and sticky. Follow the guidelines below to make sure your feedback is as helpful and productive as possible:

- **Describe the behavior you see.** "Here's what I see you doing." Remember, you may not see the whole story, but your perspective is one of the most important ones.
- **Describe the impact this behavior has.** "This is the impact I see." The behavior may affect other people, other tasks, or create a perception.
- **Make a clear request for the action you'd like the person to take. This is what you suggest they stop, start, or continue doing.** "My request is that you..." At Level 52 we use a simple three-step model for giving feedback that works well with both recognition and redirection. This model is the BID model – behavior, impact, do. Try it out. Practice. Don't be surprised if it's clunky at first.
- **Talk to your people ABOUT feedback.** Part of being a good leader is helping your people understand the importance of

feedback. Why you'll give it, how you'll give it, and that your feedback may not be great immediately, but you're working on it…

- **Be specific.** Just like in our baseball example, vague statements like, "Keep your eye on the ball" are not very helpful. Get better at very clearly stating what success looks like.
- **Show them the gap.** If the quality isn't there, show them a piece of work that operates as the right bookend and the undesirable bookend. Really invest the time in helping them see the difference between their work or behaviors and what's desired.
- **Ask for examples.** This is your metric to see how clearly you communicated. Ask them to tell you how they might do things differently next time. This not only helps you determine if they get it, but also helps them forecast and see clearly situations where they can employ the new actions.
- **What's next? Don't leave it here.** Design a plan so they know how and when you will check in with them and what they can expect you to do if you see some of the old work or behaviors pop up. Collaborate on a plan and work as a team to develop what's needed.

RECOGNIZE THE RIGHT THING

When's the last time you recognized someone on your team? Whether you call them kudos, 'atta girls, or 'atta boys, you probably know that how you recognize people, and their efforts go a long way in building a meaning-driven culture. But, like most things I tell you about in this book, there is a subtle but significant way to deliver recognition that creates more impact and meaning.

Most leaders—if they do recognize people—will recognize them for the things they did. Great job winning business, great job on the report, great job in delivering the work in a certain time period, at a certain level of quality, or for solving a specific problem for the company or the client. If you recognize something, you generally recognize those things. I want you to stop doing that.

Stop recognizing the things people do and start recognizing the behaviors that led them to do those things. They are the leading behaviors that create lagging, meaningful results.

Notice how people show up and recognize the behaviors they bring to their work. Celebrate the values they express in your culture. The resilience, the tenacity, collaboration. When you go beyond their actions or the deliverable and recognize how they behaved, this is a much deeper form of recognition that shows them that you see them as a human being and not just a human doing. It's a meaningful expression of transformational leadership rather than transactional leadership. The additional benefit of recognizing the behaviors of people is that they will start to develop consciousness around it and will want to demonstrate it more. You'll soon start to see more of those behaviors that help your team be successful. It's basically like magic that creates a warm and fuzzy kumbaya type of electric blanket that shelters you from the hard, cold streets of transactional business.

One of my team members once made a mistake that cost the business a couple thousand dollars. She knew I was going to be upset by it and came to our ensuing call prepared with a solution to ensure this mistake would never happen again. While the mistake bothered me, the behavior she exhibited was ownership and initiative. I recognized that and celebrated the hell out of it. Guess what we see more of in the business as a result. You got it. Ownership and initiative.

Give fast and furious feedback. Try the BID model and recognize the qualities you see in your people. Trust me, if you commit to the 'F' word, you will develop your people at a faster pace, they will feel valued, and you will start to see better and better results. If not, I'll buy you lunch.

SETTING PEOPLE UP FOR SUCCESS

Now that you get the inputs that help create a greater expression of your relational culture, you need to package it together to really set your people and yourself up for success. Yes, you can and should use these inputs on their own when you need to, but what becomes possible when you front-load your relationships with a wonderful collage of inputs that help people thrive from the get-go?

First, I'll tell you a story of personal failure.

I have to admit something. I fail in my leadership quite frequently. As a leader of my organization—an organization that specializes in helping people be better leaders—I fail, and it hurts when I do.

Have you ever been really excited about one of your team members and couldn't wait to see what they created? You anticipate the moment they would bust open the doors with a bounty of results, you envision hive-fives and cheers at the instant and abundant success that they would create so quickly and easily. This was the vision I had for one of my newest team members at the time. But when it came down to the first major deliverable, my experience was the opposite of celebration. I was frustrated and disappointed, and the excitement I had felt was replaced by regret. When I sat down with the team member to go over the deliverable, it was very clear immediately that I had failed as a leader. He said, "I wasn't sure if that was what you wanted, or if you'd like what I was thinking."

How could this have happened? I allowed myself to fall victim to many of the things I always tell my clients not to fall victim to:

- Letting assumptions lead the way.
- Lack of clear expectation setting.
- Having so much work that needed to be done that I basically expected this person to turn the mess into magic without taking the time to really pull the mess apart.

I failed at setting clarity and expectations, and did not set this person up for success. I hadn't bookended—I rushed everything and built a house of cards for our relationship to work on. The good thing is that you get to learn from my mistakes, so you won't have to go through the same thing.

As I shared in Chapter 3, physiologically, a cell is in either growth mode or protection mode, not in both at the same time. The people on your team and inside your organization are the same. They are either in growth mode, taking risks, pushing boundaries, and driving innovation, or they are in protection mode, working slowly and extra carefully in fear of the lashing that comes from making mistakes. People who are thrown into the fire without proper direction, clarity, and coaching tend to operate in protection mode, working from a place of fear or disappointment which will ironically lead to disappointing performance. They constantly question themselves if this is the 'right way' things need to be done or if they should just do enough to get by so expectations don't increase.

As a leader, it is your job to make sure you have created the conditions for success and individual growth. The first place you have to look when one of your people underdelivers is how you are responsible for their lack of success. What assumptions did you make? Where were you not clear? What could you have done differently? Shoot to be overly clear. Explain what needs to happen in great detail and what needs to be delivered that would truly excite you. Bookend the desirable result, for example: I want client-facing quality, I want you to be able to tell me what design principles you used and where they are, I want you to tell me what you are most excited about, I want you to tell me what you are unsure about, what you did differently from our past work, and why it's important. All of this would get me excited. Conversely, here's what would disappoint me. If you ramble on without clear messaging and direction in our conversation. If you don't take into consideration the design elements of our work.

You get the picture? The little inputs you infuse into the environment of your relationship will completely alter the expression of that person and the relationship. Are you creating an environment of growth or protection? Are you setting your team up for success?

RAT GROOMING AND ONBOARDING

We all know onboarding is important, but how important? The time spent with new team members can feel like a waste of time. With so much to get done, you'd probably like to drop a few manuals on their desk, tell them to get reading, and hope they start delivering value as soon as possible. But what if the way you onboard sets the trajectory for how people deliver value years later?

A 2004 epigenetic study led by Ian Weaver of Dalhousie University in Canada showed[18] that rats who spent more time grooming their young made those offspring braver and more resilient to stress. The baby rats actually changed their behavior due to epigenetic effects when their mother's grooming caused a particular methylation pattern in the babies' brain DNA. The changes in DNA expression occurred in the hippocampus, and as a result, those baby rats were less anxious and more well-adjusted than those rats deprived of maternal affection. You might be thinking, ok, these are rats, how does this apply to humans? A 2010 study published in the *Journal of Epidemiology and Community Health*[19] found similar results with humans. Although the brain structures and DNA expression weren't looked at specifically, the results of maternal affection at eight months of age were linked to less anxious, better adjusted adults.

What about creating the conditions for less anxious and better adjusted employees? Can leaders do subtle yet significant things that determine how an employee expresses themselves? You bet they can. I invite leaders to become relational cultural engineers. Take a stand to engineer your

---

18 Weaver, C. (2004). 'Champagne, et al. Epigenetic Programming by Maternal Behaviour.' *Nat Neurosci* (7):847–854. [Online]. Available: https://doi.org/10.1038/nn1276.

19 Mukherjee, S. (2016). 'Same but Different.' *Animals of Science,* 2 May, pp. 24–30.

environment or it will become engineered for you. Start small with the inputs that matter, and then take your engineering approach to the next level.

It all starts with onboarding. Take more time to nurture the new people on your team. Go the extra mile to over-communicate early on to ensure they have the information and context needed to be successful in your organization.

ENGINEERING RELATIONSHIPS

A lot of time and effort goes into engineering infrastructure to be efficient. A lot of time goes into engineering buildings, so they have structural integrity to handle weight and wind loads. A lot of time and energy goes into engineering software to achieve desirable performance and a high reliability product. Engineering is happening all around us, so why wouldn't you take the time and put in the effort to engineer your relationships?

It is way harder to re-engineer something later if it doesn't work. Feedback is way harder to give if you don't engineer it early on, and trust is harder to engineer after you've unintentionally broken it. Your relationships come out the gates slow and sloppy because you just haven't taken the time to do the little things that make the biggest difference.

Here's where that changes. Whether an engineer or not, you are going to pull together all of the inputs we've discussed in this chapter and use them to remove debris, reduce risk, and create a new level of meaningful performance.

WHERE ARE THE INSTRUCTIONS?

Sabrina scrunched up her nose and readjusted her glasses as she thought about her strategy. She threw her hands up in the air and said, "Ok. How do I build relationships quickly?"

Sabrina was a senior leader who had recently been promoted in an organization I was consulting for. She had taken on a new team and had new and bigger responsibilities and was feeling overwhelmed. I asked her, "What would you do if you went to IKEA and bought a new desk. You bring it home and open up the box. What's next?"

"I find the instruction manual to figure out how to put it together," she said.

Exactly. The same thing applies to building fast and strong relationships. You create and use a personal instruction manual to build a strong foundation that accelerates the way you work with others.

In 2013, I was hired to join the senior leadership team of the Coaches Training Institute in the San Francisco Bay Area. At the time a new president had come onboard to lead the organization. She sent me an email and said that she'd love to get to know me better. She also sent me a document that outlined her working preferences and asked me what my preferences were. This little exercise became a critical starting point for eliminating assumptions, and really let me know what I could, should, and shouldn't do to maximize our working relationship. It was an incredibly valuable launchpad for our relationship.

I've adapted this method into a process that I use with leaders to accelerate the foundation of their relationships through a simple six-box formula that I call the G2M, or 'Guide to Me'. Many leaders tell me that creating a personal instruction manual in itself is a really useful exercise even before they go and share it with others. I've had executive teams or new leaders use this method, and it truly creates more context for relationships and can eliminate debris that gets in the way of meaningful performance. Understanding your own preferences and sharing it with your teams prevents assumptions and creates a real strong foundation for meaningful relationships.

Where do you start when creating your G2M instruction manual? You look at these six areas: your preferences, your strengths, what drives you crazy, what you might do that drives people crazy, where things have gone wrong in the past, and the leader you aspire to be. Let's start with the first one.

YOUR PREFERENCES AND YOUR STRENGTHS

What do you know about your preferences and personality style? You've developed habits that have helped you be successful. What are they? You've developed ways of working. Whether you're an introvert, kinesthetic learner, deadline performer—whatever it is, this is an opportunity to let people know how you roll. What are your values? Giving them this information will help them to better understand how you behave and why. Are you someone who likes to close your door? Do you need time to think and process information before you answer? Perhaps you've done an assessment like Myers-Briggs, Hogan's, Enneagram, or Insights, or maybe you have information from your 360 review. What data or information can you share with your team to inform them of your preferences instead of making them guess or find out over several years?

YOUR GREATEST STRENGTHS

What are your greatest strengths, and how can people best use them? Leaders cannot be everything to everybody, so how can you share with others what the best way to use you is? How do others lean into and leverage your greatest gifts? How can you share the areas that they shouldn't lean into you for support on? For example, I've had leaders say, "You know what? I am great at 30,000-feet vision, seeing things and the way they connect with one another. Where I start to struggle is down in the details." On the flip side, you might be a leader who becomes inspired by working through the details, and you struggle with the big-picture vision. But the intent in identifying your strengths in communicating will empower people to leverage what you're great at.

WHAT DRIVES YOU CRAZY

What drives you crazy, and what should people do about it? We all have crazy makers that start as little irritations. Over time, these can develop into chronic issues if they go unaddressed. This is your chance to speak clearly and openly about those things and give others a clear heads-up as to what the impact is and how you will respond. Here's an opportunity to really get ahead of these acute pains. Whether it's people showing up late to meetings or delivering incomplete work, identify what the things are that drive you crazy, and let people know what you'd like them to do about them. Create consistency around how they can expect you to respond to these things. Make specific requests.

Below is an example of some of the things I currently have in my first three columns. You can download this template at www.level52.ca/leadershipacademy to start creating your own.

What to know about me (styles, assessments & preferences)
▪ ENTP (raging N/P). ▪ I'm a bit of a control freak. ▪ Can bypass/miss fine details. ▪ Values: Significance, connection, adventure, aliveness. ▪ Struggle with balancing time with family and work (I do well, but I struggle with it). ▪ Values in others: Brevity, creativity, resourcefulness, feedback. ▪ Interests: Broadway theatre, football, investing.

My greatest strengths & contributions
▪ Passion + Energy. ▪ Ideas – making connections between concepts. ▪ Selling. ▪ Speaking. ▪ Feedback + Growth. ▪ Collaboration. ▪ Don't ask me for help with detailed analysis. ▪ Following instruction manuals.

What drives me crazy & what to do about it
▪ Excuses: Own what you own. No bus throwing. Own your errors and move forward. ▪ AWOL: Create visibility for yourself and your work/results. ▪ Lack of Resourcefulness: I don't know how. I wasn't sure what to do. I didn't know if that's what you'd want. ▪ Late/Time: Disrespect to the time of others. On time, prepared, and ready to rock.

Guide to Me (G2M)

WHAT MIGHT DRIVE OTHERS CRAZY

The next piece requires some awareness, vulnerability, and transparency. Just like other people do things that drive you crazy, you likely do things that drive other people crazy. We all have stuff we can work on, that we're trying to get better at. Leadership isn't about perfection. It's about a continuous commitment to provide greater value.

Point out the areas you are developing. How might this impact the people you work with? What are your development habits that might frustrate people? Share them with the people that you're working with so that they know what to watch out for. This is an opportunity to enroll people to be feedback mechanisms for you. Tell them what you are working on to help you improve and create consistency.

I have never seen a perfect leader. Great leaders identify what others might struggle with and try to get ahead of the pain. It might be that unapologetic piece of your brand. Whatever it is, why not just let people know what those issues are and enroll them in the process of helping you improve?

WHAT'S GONE WRONG IN THE PAST

This is where you consider where things have gone wrong in the past and what you should do about it. Leverage past failures into wins moving forward. All of the challenges that didn't go your way previously will serve as great learning opportunities as you talk about what went wrong and create agreements to ensure they don't happen again. For example, you can talk about being blindsided by someone who left the organization unexpectedly. How do you make sure that doesn't happen in this case? What other things have gone wrong in the past that you can avoid? Bring these experiences in so that you can create context for the relationship. Remove assumptions as much as possible. Assumptions are terrible debris that get in the way of meaningful relationships and impact the performance output of your team. Eliminate assumptions by communicating clearly and asking questions to help create clarity.

THE LEADER YOU ASPIRE TO BE

What kind of leader do you aspire to be and how can others help? This is an opportunity to enroll those around you to help you grow into the leader you want to be. Share your brand promise and the associations you want them to experience. This is vulnerability and transparency with purpose, allowing you to model how to request feedback so you can build a strong, consistent brand. If you've done the brand work in the previous chapter, this is an opportunity to articulate the leader you aspire to be, what you're unapologetic about, and maybe your brand promise. Whether it's "I'm going to be the kind of leader that makes sure you leave far better than you were when you stepped into this organization," or "I'm the kind of leader that wants to have you feel like you've been pushed and you've been supported," or "I'm the kind of leader that expects you to take things and run with it, and I want you to feel like you never felt shackled while you work with me." Whatever you share, the important thing is that you get clear about what type of leader you aspire to be and articulate how people can expect you to show up as a leader, consistently.

Below is an example of some of the things I currently have in my last three columns.

What might drive YOU crazy (and what to do about it)
▪ I'm a control freak = I'm working on letting go and trusting. ▪ Big vision/shiny object: Slow me down and ensure the details are there for you. Help me see the details in the not yet formed picture. ▪ Ridiculous expectations: Hard to please, for myself and others. Build Rome in one night! ▪ ID the bad and miss the growth: Easily lock onto what isn't working or what's wrong and can miss progress.

Where things have gone wrong in the past **and how we can avoid it**
▪ Trust: What are you here for? ▪ Clarity: What we are both saying yes to. ▪ "I thought..." Communication fail. ▪ "We should..." Make a direct request. ▪ Distant: Not enough attention – ask for what you need. Hold me accountable for it. ▪ Oversell/under-deliver: I get excited and at times can oversell, and I under-deliver.

The kind of leader I aspire to be
▪ Present, passionate, and pushing you further. ▪ "It was the hardest and richest experience of my career." ▪ "I was inspired and exhausted." ▪ "I'd work with him anytime, anywhere." ▪ "I grew far more than I thought I could have."

Guide to Me (G2M)

Take the time to thoughtfully fill out the G2M and then send an email to your team or an individual to experiment with your new method. For example:

Hello team,

I am excited and thrilled to be working with a team of talented and driven leaders like all of you. It is important to get to know who each of you are and what's important to you. We all have different styles of working, and the quicker we can learn one another's styles and preferences, the quicker we will be operating as a high-functioning team.

I have attached a document that tells you a little bit about me. Consider it a guide to understand how to best work with me. I'd love it if you did the same so we can start building from a place of better understanding.

I'll be reaching out soon to find a time to connect individually.

USING YOUR GUIDE TO ME (G2M) TO ENGINEER YOUR RELATIONSHIP (ER)

You understand the tremendous thought and effort that is put into engineering bridges and software to ensure effectiveness and structural integrity. Now you're ready to put the same effort into your relationships. Unfortunately, most leaders don't, and the foundations of their relationships are built on assumptions and unarticulated expectations. Using your G2M to engineer your relationships will differentiate you.

When done well, you engage in clear agreements so that your working relationships eliminate shorthand language and assumptions, leading to met expectations and mutual success. Engineered relationships can shift organizational culture because people have the context and deep understanding as to how they can best engage with one another.

The engineered relationship is an organic agreement that changes over time as frictions emerge and success is created. It's important to engineer the relationship from the start and re-engineer frequently as needed. You always need updates to the operating system as new data influences and changes your relationship. The engineered relationship helps each involved party clarify their responsibilities and identify how they can work together most effectively. Engineering relationships significantly increase the likelihood of success.

It's important to note that a powerfully engineered relationship is not only about focusing on what you are going to achieve. It's also about how you need to create the conditions for a success to happen beyond the transactions required.

The more aware and transparent both parties are about your G2M (your preferences and pitfalls), the greater depth your reengineered relationship will have.

THE FALL OF TRUST

To trust or not to trust? We all have a way of building trust. Some people need to have it earned and some give it away like a free daily newspaper. How do you create and build trust with others? Like most things, you probably do it unconsciously, but it can be a hell of a lot easier if you put your cards on the table, clarify what it is, and what both parties should do about it.

Trust is the glue that holds people together when they need it most. In times of pressure, when people have to be at their best, they need to know that others have got their back. Great teams in sport and business cultivate environments of trust that create psychological safety.

Cultures of trust often have more creativity and collaboration. People will speak with candor and challenge one another to pursue common goals. There is more championing of one another and a strong mutual respect.

Cultures that don't have trust are usually filled with people working in silos, watching their backs and more concerned with their own interests and progression than that of the collective good. Whispers abound at the water cooler as waves of gossip take hold and spread like viruses—the company becomes more like *Game of Thrones* than a tightknit family.

In such cases, we usually bring our clients' leaders together for a day to do trust assessments on one another. This involves having them rate the level of trust they have in each person. Please note, this exercise can be a disaster if it isn't set up properly, but when it is, it is a wildly effective disruption on the path to building trust.

After each individual assesses one another, we tabulate the results and show it to them. As you can imagine, people are often horrified at the results. How could you not be if you found out that people didn't trust you? This is where you need to connect with your meaningful masochist and conjure up the mindset to do something. Challenging feedback is simply information on the path of greater understanding. It's what you do with it that matters.

After the metaphorical smack across the face this trust assessment can provide, I always point people to those things they can control. Clarify the behaviors and actions that both build and break trust. What are the things that build trust in you? Is it showing up on time, or early? Is it when people provide you with solutions before you have to ask for them? Get clear about all of the things that build trust in you. Just like bookending, you also want to shine a light on those things that break trust. What are those little things that will have you question someone's competency and intention? Excuses? Rationalizations? Throwing people under the bus? Gossip? Whatever it is, identify yours then bring them to the conversation.

Take this position: If you don't trust somebody, it's your fault. And if someone doesn't trust you, it's just as much their fault as it is yours. If they aren't giving you feedback, how are you supposed to know that what you are doing is wrong, eroding trust, and leading to poor results?

Unless you clearly create the conditions for trust to emerge by articulating your trust builders and trust breakers, you are responsible for any lack of trust. I know, you're probably shaking your fist at me. Ignorance is bliss. It's so much easier to blame other people for all the crap that's wrong, but as an epigenetic engineer of your culture, you'll own it and engage in the pain as you pursue what matters most.

FORECAST FRICTION?

If you're like me, you frequently open your weather app and look at the seven-day forecast. This provides both hope—or despair, depending on the results—but more importantly, it allows you to develop a plan of action if the forecast is correct. Your job is to identify and forecast friction.

At Level 52, we have leaders do the same thing when they are engineering relationships. What are situations that you don't want to happen? What about situations that you want to be in lockstep around? Forecast the potential friction that can occur and co-engineer how you'll navigate it together.

Great coaches in sports prepare their players through creating repetitions of challenging situations. Football, for example, is a game made up of several different situations. How you respond intentionally goes a long way towards performance. If you take this principle and apply it as a critical input that influences the expression of your people, how might you use it?

Think about some challenging situations you will likely be faced with in a specific working relationship. How do you collaborate on the collective response?

For example, how do you behave if you make a mistake? What will you do if you find a mistake or if something incorrect has been delivered to a client? How will both parties respond? How should you *not* respond? What about if you can't deliver the results within the expected timeline? What will you do? You will probably disappoint the other party and it will likely erode some trust if you don't tell them beforehand, but you should talk about what you both would do in those circumstances.

These are like fire drills, very similar to the box in your G2M that deals with the things that went wrong in the past and how you can avoid them. This is situational training at the relational level.

Think about the fire drills you want to talk about. They might differ from person to person, but you will certainly increase the likelihood of a desirable response if you talk about it in advance. Otherwise, it's a crap shoot. If your leadership strategy relies on rolling the dice, the numbers will always be against you. You might get by a few times, but the house always wins in the end.

MY JOB/YOUR JOB

What's your job? Really, if you asked the people on your team to write down their job descriptions, what would you get? Better yet, if two people wrote down what they think the other person's job is, how close would the descriptions be? Where would there be gaps in understanding?

Role clarity is a small yet significant input. Whenever we host group learning events, this is an essential part of creating psychological safety and expectations. I ask people to tell me what they think my job as the facilitator is and what they think their job as the learner is. They create two columns and list what they can think of.

Clarifying who's responsible for what

Level 52's Job	My Job

Once they're done, I ask them to tell me their understanding of my job and their job. Then I get curious.

If they tell me that their job is to be engaged, I ask them how I will know if they are engaged. I also ask them how I'll know if they aren't engaged. Then I ask them what they want me to do if I see them not engaged. It literally works like magic. It's a fast track to forming clear rules of engagement because we don't let assumptions take over and form a cloud in the space, but instead create clear expectations through role clarity.

This can be another great entry point into an engineered relationship discussion. Experiment with it. Take a team member of yours, ask them what they think your and their jobs are, and get curious about their assumptions.

OPERATION ENGINEER

The time has come. You've got the inputs that can create a powerful relational culture: listening, asking powerful questions, and creating clarity through bookending and rules of engagement. You've also developed awareness through your G2M instruction manual. Everything up until this point has prepared you for the actual engineering event. Now, like a maestro with a talented ensemble, it's your job to orchestrate these different pieces of work into a melodic and harmonious experience.

Whether you're engineering or reengineering your relationships, there are multiple ways to start. You can do it in a meeting to kick off the year. You can do it as a result of a fracture in a relationship. It is simply a matter of taking action around it. Below is an example of a message you can send to kick off the process:

"Hey [insert name], I'm learning about this concept called engineering relationships and I think there are some things that could really help us take our relationship and the team to the next level. Let me know when you have a few minutes and I'll share what I've learned so far."

The best place to start is to ask the other person to take you through their G2M. As they share it, ask questions to clarify terms and expressions. Share your G2M and invite them to ask questions to gain deeper clarity. Use the inputs discussed in this chapter, get curious, and engineer a strong foundation for your relationship. There is a great roadmap for you to download at www.level52.ca/leadershipacademy.

A great engineered relationship will activate a new level of performance and will give the people on your team the space to take ownership.

CREATE OWNERSHIP

How do I drive bigger and better results this year without making my employees feel like disposable pawns on my chessboard as I constantly try to get more and more out of them?

Work can be monotonous. Many people feel like they're lined up at a factory as they step into unsatisfying roles in unsatisfying jobs. And archaic goal setting and performance management can reinforce an uninspired clock-punching mentality, adding to the tragic statistic of the overwhelmingly actively disengaged workforce around the world. Whether you are there or not, we will now explore how one simple question can transform the engagement of a company to create an inspired workforce that delivers better results.

The question is, what will make this year the best year of your professional career?

First, let's talk about the problem with most goal setting. I've seen it in organizations everywhere. Unfortunately, most goal setting doesn't work. Usually it's a poor version of smart goals based on a slight increase of last year's performance but has nothing to do with what an individual is actually capable of. Most individual contributors and leaders rush through the process of goal setting so they can get back to their 'real work'. As a result, the foundational aspect of your yearly performance is already off to a rocky start as it simply turns into a management practice to appease senior management. This may not be everybody, but it happens more than you think, and it isn't even the biggest problem.

In the next chapter, we'll talk about the mechanics of goals themselves and how you can create engagement and results simply through clarity and feedback. But there's an even bigger shift that must occur if you want to lift the lid on the upcoming year. Current goal setting, for the most part, focuses simply on the output of the individual with little regard for the inputs that create the fuel to drive their engine.

You likely tend to focus on what value you are going to create for the business, which isn't bad. It's necessary to keep the lights on and the doors open. But what if you can do it better? And you can. The people on your team, the employees in your company, all of us are creatures of repetition. And the repetition we are exposed to in our day-to-day interactions shapes how we see the world.

If I'm on your team and you are constantly asking me about what I'm delivering, what my results are, and what the progress on a task is, it can create a big disconnect between who I am and what I value because you're putting a sharp focus purely on what you need from me and what I'm producing for the business. Now, you might be sitting there reading this, thinking, "Well, of course! That's what I'm paying you to do," and there's some truth to that. But you also have to understand that if you continue to look at it that way, you are an active contributor to an actively disengaged workforce that produces only a fraction of their potential value. It's simply a bad investment.

What if you can actually enhance the results by creating an input that focuses on what is most important to the individual across the table from you? I'm telling you, the leaders who do are surprised at the immediacy of the impact when they shift the focus to what fulfills people, what mark they want to make on the business, and what their legacy might be. Whether you like it or not, big or small, we will all leave a legacy in our business. So why not make it intentional?

Here's why this one question is important. I'll create some context by referencing some of the great work Marshall Goldsmith has done, which he refers to in his book *Triggers: Creating Behavior That Lasts—Becoming the Person You Want to Be.*[20] Most of you have been exposed to an engagement survey in some way. These surveys usually include some common questions that are indicators of a culture that has highly engaged individuals. For example, questions like: Do I have clear goals? Do I have close relationships? Do I have the resources I need to be successful? Generally, if people answer yes to these questions, it's an indicator that you have an engaged workforce. Now, Marshall Goldsmith asks, "What if the questions are problematic and they themselves contribute to a disengaged

---

20 Goldsmith, M. (2016) *Triggers*. Profile Books Ltd.

workforce?" He creates a distinction between passive and active questions. A lot of the engagement surveys out there actually reinforce a passive work environment where the people in your organization are victims to their environment.

So, what if we tweaked the questions?

Instead of asking: Do you have clear goals?

Ask: Do you do your best to make sure you have clear goals? Do you do your best to build strong relationships at work? Do you make sure you have the resources you need to be successful?

It's a slight tweak in how the question is asked that has a significant impact on shaping whether or not people are passive victims of the environment or active participants responsible for creating it.

What will make this year the best year of your professional career?

Why is this question so powerful? First of all, it gives you incredible insight into what is important to the person in front of you, what excites them, what they want to reach, what risks they might want to take, where they might want to get different exposure, what they want to do more or less of. And if you step in with genuine curiosity, you can learn a lot about what drives this individual. You can start to collaborate around how you might be able to reach these goals together. This in itself has a big impact that shows them you believe in them and their development and that their passion is paramount to the success inside the organization. When you do this, you will get more from them.

In highly transactional environments, people will generally hang their hat on two things: Am I getting better compensation, and am I getting a better title? They have nothing else to grab hold of. By asking, what will make this year the best year of your professional career? You start to pay attention to the person and who they are developing into. You invest energy towards their growth that may have no relation to a compensation bump or a fancy title but presents a true opportunity to develop and shift the trajectory of their career.

This question is the starting point. What you ask afterwards will deepen and add value as you make them active participants in creating the best year of their professional career. If this was the best year of your professional career, what would you create? What risks would you take? A year from now, what is it that you did you would be most excited about? After you explore with them the feeling, the excitement that they'll feel after their best year, you can shift to some goal setting activities. Ask, in order to achieve this, what would you have to do that's different to create these different results? Help them identify these actions.

You also need to help them identify the new behaviors they'll need. How will you have to BE different in order to make this real? Whether it be demonstrating more courage, resilience, or collaboration, what are the behavioral shifts you'll need to make to truly drive the actions you mentioned? As their leader, identifying these behavior shifts helps you create the frame for them to make this the best year of their career. In your one-on-one meetings you can keep coming back to how they are making that happen and design how you can provide feedback. Remember how important feedback is? Just wait, there's more in the next chapter.

What if, every year, a key goal for you as a senior leader was helping others create the best year of their professional career? Why not have that as your key orientation point? This doesn't mean you can necessarily cater to everyone's wants and needs, but it's a great starting point. There will be times that you're disappointed, but why wouldn't you try to block and tackle for them as best you can to help them create that? They will be highly engaged team members.

You can elevate the question even further. After they've explored their best year and identified the necessary actions and behaviors, you help them design how you can best support them. What do I need to do differently in order to help you create this? Maybe you need to get out of the way. Maybe they need more hand-holding. So often people make assumptions in how they should work with others, and they don't ask. Ask them, what do I need to do differently in order to help you create this? How will I need to be different in order to help you create this? Do I need to push you more? Do I need to hold them more accountable? Do I need to champion you? It's your job to pull this out of them so that you can help them to create the best professional year of their career. This is an opportunity for them to engineer you as a leader for how to work best with them.

Whether or not you have set your goals yet, grab a coffee with someone on your team, have a breakfast meeting, whatever. Take the time to connect with each person on your team and start by asking them this question: What would make this the best year of your professional career? Then be curious and ask follow-up questions. You will create more resonance, a clear frame, and an opportunity for them to look at the year differently than the previous year. This will enhance results by creating more fulfilment and a self-driven culture of performance. Plus, this is a great starting point to engineer or reengineer your relationship. You can download and complete our worksheet of supporting questions to help you navigate this question with yourself and the people on your team. You'll find it at www.level52.ca/leadershipacademy.

How do I drive bigger and better results without making my employees feel like pawns? The answer is by harnessing their hearts and minds through connecting with the person, understanding what they value, what they want, and how they think they can get there. If you get them aimed at creating a fulfilling experience, they will take risks and push boundaries, creating the bridge between high engagement and exceptional results. That is the expression every leader should want and can truly create with their people. It is meaningful leadership.

I've spent most of my time in this chapter giving you strategies to create the conditions for successful team and relational cultures. Now, in part two, I'm going to take this a layer outward and look at the larger organizational culture as a whole. It's one thing to engineer a relationship, but how do you engineer an organizational culture?

PART TWO: EPIGENETICS AND YOUR ORGANIZATIONAL CULTURE

What's more important, finding the right job, or the right culture?

I have a friend who is a real high performer in her industry—an exceptional talent. We got together over a cup of coffee to discuss her career, as she was exploring her next opportunity. I asked her, if she could move into any industry or step into any role, what would excite her the most?

Her answer wasn't what I was expecting, and it was brilliant. She said, "To be honest, I'd rather pick a culture than a job." She was working as a contractor for a large organization at the time and was quickly shifted from the contract she was hired to do and placed in a different area because she was delivering great results. Delivering great results was the easy part. The hard part was the culture. She started working in a lethargic, unimaginative group, which consisted of your classic paycheck collectors. They'd push back whenever improvements were suggested because, well, it would simply mean more work. She was acutely aware of the dangers of staying in an environment like that. It doesn't matter how much talent or motivation you have. If you swim in a pool long enough with people who are only concerned about their own self-interests, an easy workload, and consistent paychecks, it's not going to be fulfilling. And worse, over time, you might become one of those people. I see this in poor cultures where people are compensated handsomely with little accountability.

Why would it make sense to pick a great culture and an unfamiliar role over the perfect role in a terrible culture? The perfect role in a terrible culture is like an invitation to a really bad party. That's right, it's labelled a party, but you'll spend most of your time frustrated at the attitudes and negativity around you. It will eventually penetrate you, and over time you will become a susceptible host to those viruses and behaviors, taking on much of that negativity yourself and spreading it unconsciously. You'll start to embody it, making you less effective and less employable, and you'll develop the habits and mindset that people don't want. I have seen it for myself. Talented people who come in hungry, who are motivated, who come to do good but quickly find out that there's no accountability and are then spoiled in the poor environment. They come to do good and then stay to do well.

In a great culture, you will learn rapidly. You will be challenged and inspired by those you work with. It will become a community that collectively raises the tide and grows individuals beyond what they thought they were capable of.

There is a specific type of bird that is very valuable because of the beautiful sound it makes. Initially, scientists thought that this was just the nature of the bird, but then they studied it and found that if average birds were placed in the same cage as these beautiful, singing, prized possession birds, the mediocre birds would start to sing the same tune. This singing bird effect unfortunately goes both ways. More often than not we put prized birds in a terrible environment with an overwhelming sound of negativity. Soon, the unbearable music becomes an addictive behavior inside the organization.

I simplify culture as being the mosaic of mindsets that infuse the environment with specific behaviors and artifacts. It's always evolving based on the inputs that create the quality of the environment that your people swim in. Leaders who truly own their organizational culture are very aware of the elements that contribute to or detract from it. Garbage in, garbage out.

Become aware of the environment you're creating or allowing to be created. If someone like this high performing friend of mine walks in the door seeking a culture, what would she say about yours? Would she jump at the chance or run away, even if it's the perfect role?

THE VALUE OF HONESTY IN CULTURE

Culture can remain elusive and frustrating when there are different meanings and interpretations amongst senior leaders in an organization.

What will happen if you get your leaders in the same room and ask them how the company is doing when it comes to culture? Do you see things the same way? Are you looking through the same frame? Chances are, the answer is no. Culture is often elusive because you can't achieve the aspired culture if you don't share the same clarity of what the culture could and should be.

For example, you might be able to name your organization's guiding principles or core values, and everyone on the team might have the same general understanding, but in my experience, there will likely be small differences in how they are perceived. These differences create gaps and misalignment on how you all collectively drive and support the culture you want.

If you are doing a culture assessment with your leaders, start with defining your values. Are they words on a wall—drive-by values—or are they the key indicators of your culture?

Go through the list of values and bookend them. For example, take a core value of truth and honesty and define it. What is a poor expression of truth and honesty? What is the desired expression of truth and honesty? It's this simple input that will have significant results.

This, like all thing's leadership, comes down to intentionality and practice.

UNDERSTANDING YOUR ORGANIZATIONAL CULTURE

Before you can engineer your organizational culture, you should take a step back and assess its current state. You could engage in a long and expensive culture assessment, run an engagement survey, or simply take the first step of downloading and completing our one-page culture scan. This culture scan involves having some of your leaders capture data during their work for a month and bringing it together for an offsite to make meaning of it.

We use a method adapted from Johnson and Scholes's Cultural Web

Model to examine your environment.[21] We look at the following things: What are the stories that are told at meetings, at the water cooler, or at past events? How are people talked about, inside and outside of the company? Who and what the company chooses to create a narrative around is a strong indicator of what it values and what it perceives as most important. So, what are those stories?

After you've explored your environment's narratives, take a walk around your office. What are the symbols you see? It can be the colors, the attire people wear, the signage, the furniture. Maybe even the unique jargon that is used inside your organization. These are all symbols that are a reflection of your culture.

Then, of course, there are behaviors. What are the daily and weekly behaviors and actions that you observe inside the pool that your people swim in? This determines what happens in given situations. How do your people respond? What are the general behaviors? The common behaviors or actions in the environment are indicators of what your culture is.

The last indicator relates to the roles and controls in the environment. This includes both the roles defined by the organizational chart as well as the unwritten lines of responsibility. What are these roles? What are the expected outcomes, and how is accountability controlled?

If people have a problem, where do they go? Do they line up outside your office, for example? This could indicate that there is a culture of deferring to authority in your organization.

This culture scan is a great place to start understanding your organizational culture. It will help you see what is working really well in your environment and where you need to infuse better inputs.

When you get the culture right, everyone will want to swim in your pool.

---

21 Johnson and Scholes. (1992). The Cultural Web Model. *BusinessBalls*. [Online]. Available: www.businessballs.com/strategy-innovation/cultural-web-johnson-scholes/.

ENGINEER YOUR ENVIRONMENT OR IT WILL ENGINEER YOU

Are cultures formed on their own or do you play a part in how they are shaped?

Think about a group of people living on a remote island. They have limited contact with the outside world, and their cultural practices are consistent with the way they have been for centuries. This is not a fabricated situation. There are still such cultures out there, like the fascinating story of the Sentinelese of North Sentinel Island.[22] Although it's technically part of the Republic of India, you'll be met by a barrage of arrows if you try and get near the island.

Due to limited exposure to the outside world, for better or worse, such cultures are very distinct and are constantly reinforced through the tribal practices and accepted rituals. The leaders are the custodians of that culture, constantly reinforcing the good and course-correcting the undesirable to get the epigenetic expression of the culture you want.

As a leader of your organization, you have a tough job. You aren't isolated like the Sentinelese but you must be the gatekeeper for the behaviors and guiding principles you let on your island and what you let stay. If you aren't intentional and vigilant about protecting what's important—guess what? You'll likely have nice words on the wall and a fancy mission statement, but incongruence when it comes to the behaviors that are expressed.

So, do cultures happen, or do you happen to create culture? One of my executive clients once shared with me a conversation he had with a board member who criticized him for putting so much effort into culture. This board member told my client that cultures form on their own, so he shouldn't waste his time trying to build it.

What's the alternative? Should you just hope the right culture is formed?

---

22 Misra, K.K. (2016). 'The Sentineles of Andaman and Nicobar Islands.' *The Particularly Vulnerable Tribal Groups in India: Privileges and Predicaments*. Anthropological Survey of India, pp. 659–668.

Or do you focus on creating the culture you want? It's probably no surprise to you that I take a stand for leaders to practice extreme intentionality—to do their best to engineer the cultures they want and relentlessly reinforce the cultural principles that lead to organizational success. This way, leaders at least have a chance to deliberately shape the behaviors, mindsets, and norms that lead to a meaningful and effective culture.

Meaning-driven leaders obsess over the little things that make a difference. In this case, the things that enhance or detract from our culture—the things that strengthen or put the business at risk. It's not a capability issue, but an environmental one. For example, a culture of feedback won't happen on its own if you don't point, reward, and recognize people for delivering it.

The belief that cultures form on their own probably comes from an unwillingness to identify what the culture is and what you want it to be. It's harder to focus on the invisible force that fuels expression than it is the lagging results created by it. The pursuit of greater understanding can help you create meaning from the otherwise meaningless.

CREATING THE CONDITIONS FOR COLLABORATION

By now, you know the power of high-impact questions but probably still filter performance through the lens of your expertise and the way you must harness people's ability to drive results. What if you created the conditions for success and then completely got out of the way?

Educational researcher Sugata Mitra conducted a fascinating 'hole in the wall'[23] experiment that showed how the right conditions can lead to collaboration and success. He looked out the window of his office in New Delhi and asked himself how many developers were out there in the slums that didn't have the chance to learn. So he embedded a computer

23 Mitra, S. (2005). 'Self-Organising Systems for Mass Computer Literacy: Findings From the "Hole in the Wall" Experiments.' *International Journal of Development Issues,* 4(1):71–81. [Online]. Available: https://www.emerald.com/insight/content/doi/10.1108/eb045849/full/html.

in the side of a building in a slum. Children immediately surrounded it. Uneducated and barely speaking English, they got curious about what this thing in the wall was. Mitra connected the computer to high-speed Internet and left it there. What happened? The kids who wanted to learn about the computer spent countless hours learning how to work it and taught their peers how to work it too. Through self-driven learning in the right conditions, children with no knowledge of computers were able get to the same level of computer acumen as an educated office administrator could within a few months. Mitra is set to prove that self-organizing systems can develop emergent knowledge with little to no influence from the outside.

Little things, like getting out of the way, can make a significant difference to performance. Mitra's approach helped shape the method we use at Level 52 to shift cultures of top-down decision-making and create the conditions for innovation, while leveraging the talent and intellectual capability of those in the business.

Think about a problem you need to solve. If you are like most leaders we work with, you can spend countless hours agonizing over creating a solution to your biggest problems. What if I told you that you didn't have to?

Right now, think about some of the biggest problems you face. It might be reducing costs. It might be activating the engagement of your people. Perhaps it's cracking the code on developing a culture of accountability.

Whatever it is, it shouldn't be your problem to solve.

What if the solution to your biggest problems was you getting out of the way?

It will be hard to do—remember you love being an expert and having all of the answers—so you are going to have to employ some sort of creative constraint. A creative constraint is an innovation principle that removes important elements you rely on, forcing you to explore and develop something different. For example, when someone has a stroke, the quickest way to rehabilitate a paralyzed limb is to remove the ability to use the fully functioning limb. By removing the ability to use the healthy limb, you force the individual to go through the painful struggle of learning, or relearning in this case, to accelerate the rehabilitation.

When it comes to solving the problems of your organization, you are the metaphorical limb that's relied on most. People come to you and you fret over solving their problems, when you are likely to get a better result AND more engagement when you create the conditions for the problem to be solved instead by activating the epigenetic expression of your team. You can do this by learning how to hack sprint your problems.

A hack sprint is a fast-paced collaboration that leverages the intellectual capability of your people. It's an intentionally designed and rapid collaboration that seeks to answer a problem, challenge, or deficit.

Your job as the leader is to focus on really defining the problem that needs to be solved and then to find the key data points that will inform your people as to what's important. Then you throw them in teams and watch them build a workable model to solve the problem.

We've done hack sprints with leaders in many different industries to identify new ways of adding value, capture market share, and significantly reduce cost of goods. Leaders are often shocked at the results their people come up with when we give them full permission to get creative and share what they see. You need to get out the way and let them do it.

At the end of a hack sprint, most leaders are not only ecstatic about the solutions presented, but they remark how they are already ahead of the game when it comes to leading the change initiative because they have a group of change champions who are already invested in the outcome.

So, how do you hack sprint?

First, define the problem into a How Might We (HMW) statement:

How might we reduce costs by two million dollars this year?
How might we increase market share by X% this year?
How might we reduce attrition by X% this year?

The HMW question has a specific goal in mind.

Then give participants the relevant data points that will give them insight into their solution. Such as, what we spent and where we spent it. You may want to have subject matter experts (SMEs) provide brief presentations on the relevant information.

Next, set the criteria for the hack sprint. For example:

- The amount of time they'll have to collaborate and present a model that can be actioned quickly.
- The amount of money you are willing to invest.
- The time period from launch to finish.
- Bonus points for creativity or disruptive solutions.

Your number-one job in this process is to get out of the way once the HMW question and criteria have been set. Don't get sucked into discussions where people will take your perspective—that defeats the purpose. Your job is to roam and spot the behaviors you want to see. Recognize people for their collaboration, notice when they ask great questions, look through the lens of your organizational values, and recognize those when you see them.

Then, sit back and watch the creativity of the teams as they compete to be the winners. Sometimes organizations offer a prize, but really, for the most part, people love being a part of the solution.

Empowering your people to collaborate is key to creating the conditions for success, helping you get ahead of the curve when it comes to innovating your business before it takes a nightmare to wake you up.

ENGINEERING CERTAINTY IN UNCERTAIN TIMES

What can leaders do when market conditions are dire and distracting? When people lose focus and become scared? In these situations, the chatter inside organizations is mostly about fear, uncertainty, job cuts. The list goes on. How do you stop that? What can you do to prevent negativity from spreading through the organization like a virus?

When we're asked to come in and work with organizations facing such challenges in their environment, we go through a step-by-step process of identifying concerns and reframing uncertainty with them. It starts with asking some simple questions.

First of all, I ask them to give me all the reasons that upcoming year will be the same as the previous year. At first, I always get some pushback. Something like, "Well, it won't be. It just won't be." That's when I say, "Okay, maybe that's true, but give me the reasons why it will be. You just need to work a little harder to find out what those reasons are." After some prodding and encouragement, teams always come up with a solid list of reasons that could influence why that year would be the same as the previous year. That's step one.

Next, I ask teams, "Give me all the reasons why this year will be *worse* than last year." You can imagine the energy in the room and how easy it is for people to come up with perceived barriers and obstacles.

I then go on to the next step. "Give me all the reasons why this year will be better than last year." Once the teams come up with some reasons, I ask the last question, "Give me all the reasons why this year is going to be the best year yet."

I then display the resulting list of possible outcomes on the wall so everyone can look at them together, and I ask them which result they think is the most likely. I find that, at this point, the vast majority of people tend to be optimistic that that year would be better than the previous one. Despite the uncertain marketplace, going through these thought exercises will usually have them all looking in the same direction, their negativity abated.

But this is only the beginning. The reality is that all of these results—the same as last year, worse, better or the best year yet—are possible. The outcome depends on how we frame it and what we do in our daily, weekly, and monthly interactions to make it real. This requires some deeper work.

To kick that off, I ask groups to look at the upcoming year's obstacles, fears, and concerns and identify which of those they are the most concerned about. I give them the opportunity to just put it all out on the table. Once they have all their concerns down, I introduce the mindfulness concept—what you focus your attention on will expand. Trust me, as a high performance athlete, I spent many years focusing on what was wrong. And what expanded in me? Well, the things that weren't working. There are, of course, benefits to focusing on problems if you want to make improvements, but overall, if you look from a leadership perspective, if you're constantly focusing on what's not working, what you're concerned about, it will expand. It will take over and become a powerful, deflating narrative inside the organization. I'm constantly working on improving the habit of mindfulness. What you focus on expands. So, what is it that you want to expand?

The next step is around self-awareness. I ask teams, "As a leader, what do you know about how you deal with uncertainty?" Try it now. Think about a time when you faced uncertainty. It doesn't matter if it was personal or professional. How did you deal with it? How did you respond? How did you react, deal with others, support others?

This also ties in with your internal locus of control. "Given the current situation, what can you control?" Did you know that there is a Chinese symbol that is the same for crisis and opportunity? Any time we're faced with something, it also provides an opportunity to expand, grow, pivot, or point us in a different direction. You understand that a cell is either in growth mode or protection mode, so where do you want to choose to be? Are you in a position to spot opportunities for growth? The opportunity lies in reframing the current situation around the crisis or uncertainty and rallying the team around it. This is when a leader should say, "Yeah, you know what? It's tough out there, but this is also a great opportunity for us to be the last one standing."

Most innovation is a result of a crisis. Deviance breeds innovation. When unexpected circumstances shake the foundation that you stand on, you can either adapt and innovate or slowly die as you lament how hard things are now and how things used to be. It's an easy trap to fall into. It just won't get you anywhere.

Once I've worked on the mindset to navigate uncertainty with teams, I personalize it by asking, "What do you want to be known for when it comes to dealing with uncertain times?" What behaviors will you express and how will you deal with the conversations that can become downward spirals? This brings us back to the leader brand. What are the associations you want people to make based on how you engage with them? What is the legacy, the reputation that you're crafting with intentionality? Will your peers remember you for the great qualities that you demonstrated when faced with uncertainty? The confidence you put into the team, choosing to lead and reframe the current situation from a crisis into an opportunity?

The final piece of this process can be a critical input when it comes to navigating uncertainty. This is where I ask teams, "What does it take to win?" We're all going to be faced with losses, whether big or small, but what does it take to win? If you break down the word WIN into an acronym, it becomes three words that will always point you in the right direction (This is something that several successful sport teams employ.) It doesn't matter if you just lost a big client. It doesn't matter if you just had a touchdown scored over top of you. Those three words are: What's Important Now?

How do you take whatever situation you're faced with now, grow, develop, and continue to move the ball down the field?

Create something certain. And how does a leader create certainty when faced with uncertainty? Well, that certainty comes from where you point people to look, through the questions you ask. Invite them to step into the place of self-authorship. Connect them with their internal locus of control to create something certain—something that lies within their circle of influence.

Continue to orient yourself and your team to the opportunities that can be created in times of crisis and uncertainty. This is when you masterfully engineer and influence multiple levels of culture at the same time to get the greater expression of your people.

CONCLUSION

Too often, organizations get bogged down by the genetic joke, believing that their success or failure is predetermined by their blueprint—the strategy, rules, and conventions that guide them. But just as in nature, where epigenetics determines how DNA is expressed, your organization's expressions will also be determined by how your blueprint is communicated and the external and internal environment of the organization. As a leader, it's your responsibility to understand the inputs that affect this environment. The inputs that determine the expression of your personal, team, and organizational cultures.

In this chapter, we looked at some practical tools and exercises you can use to engineer and improve your relationships and culture on the team and organizational level. By applying these tools proactively and consistently, you can engineer your organization's environment to set your team up for success and growth, even when faced with uncertainty.

THINGS TO REMEMBER

- Epigenetics is the science that explains why culture eats strategy for breakfast.
- Blueprints are nothing more than a plan. It's how the plan is executed that matters.
- You are responsible for three layers of culture: your own, your team, and your organizational culture.

- Inputs affect the expression of the DNA in each environment. What inputs matter?
- Relational inputs that matter: listening, high-impact questions, bookending clarity, trust, role clarity, and engineering relationships.
- The small inputs into your culture can have a significant impact on the expression of your people. Once you are aware you are responsible for everything, you are responsible for everything.

CREATE MEANING

Awareness: What inputs are affecting the expression of myself, my team, and my organization?

Intention: What intentional inputs will transform your culture from slow, sloppy, and isolated to a greater expression of the talent?

Exercise: Identify a relationship to re-engineer. Send your 'guide to me' to the other person as a starting point and get together, get curious, and seek to learn their instruction manual.

Reflection: Set up a time to reflect and assess how you listened with a discovery and empathetic focus. How were your high-impact questions?

6

GAMING YOUR GROWTH

OLD DOGS AND NEW TRICKS

Breaking inertia can be the hardest part of any transformation. How do you get the ball rolling and get momentum on your side? Sometimes it can feel impossible but breaking through inertia is where it all starts.

One of my clients, a large global organization, recently faced this problem when they promoted their CFO, Doug, to the position of COO.

"I obviously need to change to be successful in this role," Doug said to me.

You see, Doug had been thrust into this new role after the retirement (possibly forced) of his predecessor and was suddenly tasked with new responsibilities that required a different skill set.

As part of his transition, Level 52 ran a 360 assessment so he could get honest and direct feedback on how his direct reports, peers, and boss perceived him. While the results confirmed Doug's competence in several areas, there were some big flashing lights when it came to identifying opportunities to improve.

Doug had been very effective as a CFO. He knew the numbers inside and out and was trusted as the holder of company financials. In a senior position in an industry that was undergoing significant challenges, he had to be on top of his game. The benefits of his expertise were clear. Financial accuracy was paramount, and he was the gatekeeper to what initiatives could or couldn't be done. The downside of his relentless pursuit of financial fervor was the reputation he developed over the years as a reductionist grim reaper—someone who always defaulted to the numbers because really, nothing else mattered.

This 360 came as a wake-up call to Doug. In debriefing the report, we discussed what needed to be different moving forward.

"Look," he said, "I'm on the back nine of my career, and while we can sit here and talk about fluffy stuff and what I need to do differently, can you really teach an old dog new tricks?"

This is a great question. I can answer it with confidence, but it depends on many things coming together to facilitate a transformation.

What does Doug do? Will Doug take the path of least resistance, hop onto the golf cart and cruise through the final holes of his career? Using the same technique and playing proverbial whack-a-mole on his way to the final putt? Or will Doug clean his clubs, fix his technique, and redefine his game so he can change his destiny? Can this old dog learn new tricks?

I love cliffhangers. We are going to give Doug a break so you and I can explore the wonders of the brain and this little thing called myelin. At the end of this chapter, you'll understand why it's so hard to change. As challenging as change can be, the structures you'll learn in this chapter will help you focus your attention on the right things to help you and the people who work with you get better, faster.

ME-O MYELIN

Shortly after I turned 16, I bought a Nissan Sentra from my sister when she upgraded to something more prestigious. It was a farm car that had over 200,000 miles on it. A little bit rusty, but otherwise a reliable A to B car. Perfect for my first vehicle. Well, almost perfect, except for the standard transmission. Learning how to drive a car is hard enough as it is but learning how to drive a standard is slightly more challenging. The timing of the clutch, moving the gears into place, the grinding that quickly alerts you that you're doing it wrong, the jerky motion as you seek to find the elusive sweet spot of releasing the clutch and giving the car more gas, and to top it off, your mother screaming through it all: NO, NOT LIKE THAT JAY! DO IT LIKE THIS! NO. NOPE! NOT LIKE THAT. SHEEESH!

Stressful. But would you believe it? After hours and hours of practice, I transformed from a shaky learner into a well-adapted, quasi-professional driver. My mother's screaming was replaced by the loud volume of Garth Brooks, eating a cheeseburger, and talking to my friends, all while driving. It's amazing that now I can drive home safely and not have much of a recollection of how I got there. It's like muscle memory, or from a neuroscience perspective, automaticity. How does this happen?

Since the introduction of fMRI scanning (functional magnetic resonance imaging) in the 1990s, we've been invited to a deep and unending exploration of the intricacies of the brain and have come to better understand how it works—at least we think we do. To understand the development and acquisition of any skill, it helps to understand what myelin is and why it matters.

Simply put, myelin is the physiological indicator of skill. It's the sausage-shaped layer of dense fat that wraps around nerve fibers and speeds up the transmission of neural activity. Envision a copper wire and the rubber casing that surrounds it. Without the rubber casing, the electricity could leak out, causing delays and slowing transmission. Just like the casing prevents the electrical impulse from leaking out, myelin provides your neurons' casing that leads to faster and more efficient impulses. The more layers of myelin, the stronger the signal and the faster things move. A neurologist would be able to see the layers of myelin in the regions of your brain correlated with those skills you are good at.

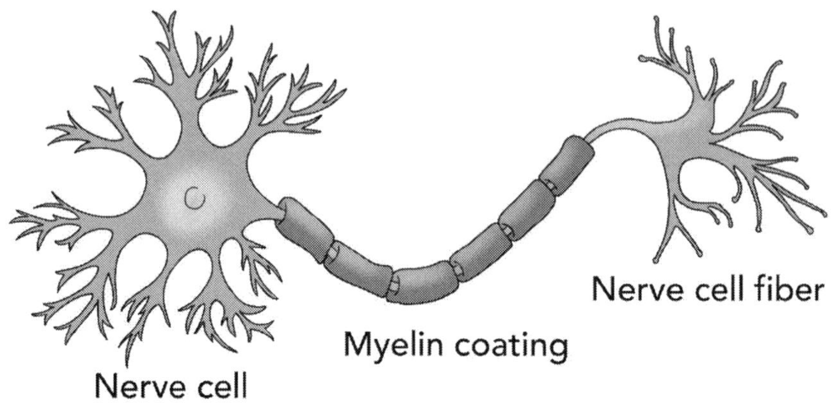

Myelin around a nerve fiber

The less myelin you have, the harder things are and the more thought, time, and energy they require—like a learner driver white-knuckling the steering wheel of his car. The more myelin you have, the less thought, time, and energy is required, like driving with your knee as you eat a cheeseburger and sing your favorite song. Myelin is mastery, and it's your job to accelerate the growth of myelin in the areas that matter.

How do you grow myelin? I'll explain by adapting Daniel Coyle's ingredients for myelin growth as outlined in his book, *The Talent Code*.[24] Those ingredients are struggle, repetition, and engagement.

STRUGGLE

"I've already tried that."

This statement invites the wrath of Jayson. It doesn't matter if it's one

---

24 Coyle, D. (2010). *The Talent Code: Unlocking the Secret of Skill in Maths, Art, Music, Sport, and Just About Everything Else.* Arrow.

of my kids or one of my clients saying it. Somewhere along the path of development from child to adult, you start rationalizing your inability to achieve something. You shrug your shoulders and give yourself a pat on the back for a single attempt that yields a disappointing result. The problem comes in when you accept the disappointing result. You might say something like, "That's not my thing," or "Yeah, that doesn't work." All of these are unconscious statements that might let your ego off the hook. But those of us in the know can see right through you. Yes, I'm pointing at you. Don't be lazy. Stop using that statement, and let's get serious about myelinating what's important to you.

You know already from Chapter 3 that no pain means no gain and that struggle is a biological requirement for growth. Our brains are mechanisms of efficiency. They are designed to govern the flow of resources and make critical decisions as to where and how the energy is spent based on activity. The brain trims unused connections so it can allocate more attention and resources to the systems that are being used, reinforcing them. This means that newer pathways require more thought, effort, and energy. That's why new things are hard. It's supposed to be.

To help you understand why it's so frustrating to get better at something, I'll introduce you to the four learning steps that explain how we learn as adults.

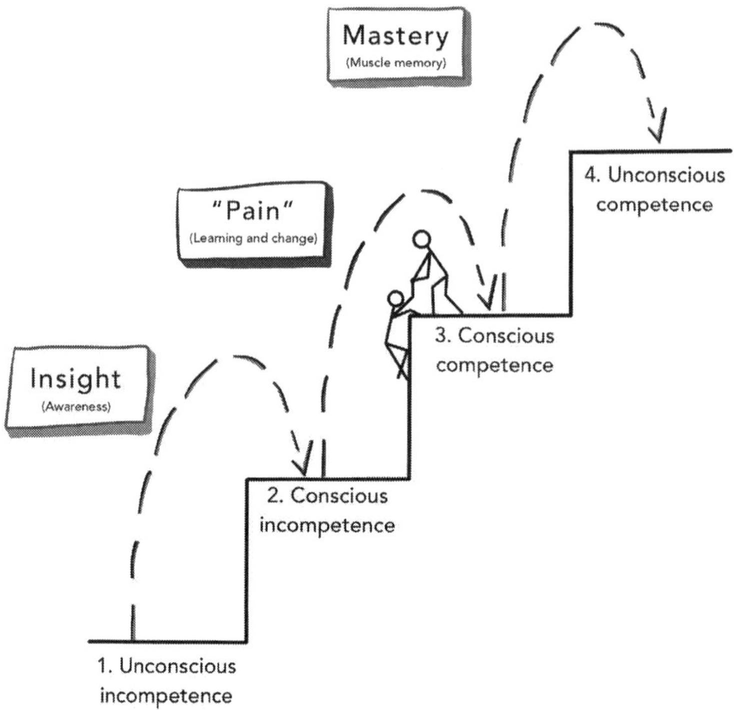

The four adult learning steps

Step one is called **unconscious incompetence**: This is the easiest step because you have no idea what you don't know. You aren't even aware of it, therefore you have no idea or concern about doing it. It's the classic example of ignorance is bliss. Remember when, as a kid, your parents would drive you somewhere, and you'd just magically show up at locations almost like a teleporter sent you there? Unconscious incompetence.

Step two is **conscious incompetence**: This is the step that hits you like a sledgehammer. You are now aware of what's needed, and the incredible amount of resources required to get over the massive skill gaps to achieve your desired results. It's hard and painful, and you feel as useless as a one-legged man in an ass-kicking competition. Your parents finally let you practice and you white-knuckle that steering wheel, look two inches in front of the car, and flex your butt every time you get within 10 feet of another vehicle. It takes incredible focus, effort, and energy.

Step three is **conscious competence**: This is the step where things start clicking for you. You see things and then do what you are supposed to do. It still takes some effort, but you also get some internal rewards when you see your efforts deliver what's intended. You see growth, you see progress, and all that pain and suffering suddenly feels worth it. After you've been driving for a while, you can shoulder check when changing lanes, can pull off a reasonable parallel park, and can get safely from point A to B without risking your life.

Step four is **unconscious competence:** This is the place of mastery. You seem to possess an incredible ability to do things remarkably well with no effort. It's like being able to safely drive your car with one knee on the steering wheel while taking a bite out of your cheeseburger and chatting to your best friend on Bluetooth. You navigate through rush hour traffic flawlessly and arrive home not really knowing what route you took home. Unconscious competence requires very little thinking, and at this level, you can demonstrate great skill with less effort.

Understanding the steps involved in improving at anything can provide some context around the discomfort we experience when learning something new. Especially if you are an adult who has been successful at certain things and now find yourself in a situation that's new and it feels like you're trying to lift a 400-pound weight in your organization.

What is your equivalent of a 400-pound power clean? Is it mastering financial acumen and understanding the levers that impact margins? Is it dealing with a difficult team member? Collaborating with peers? Presenting to large audiences? Whatever it is, the struggle is real, and the real part about it is the opportunity to get better when you commit to improving. Identifying it as a struggle is one thing, but connecting it to your brand and legacy can keep you going so you get your critical reps in. The important thing is to keep going. At least on those things that are important to you.

When you understand that struggle is an indicator of greener and greater myelination pastures, you can approach it differently. Rather than just accepting that you or someone on your team is simply 'bad at something,' you just need to myelinate it. Rather than seeing a new change initiative as bad or hard, see the struggle as an important first step in the process of myelination. Neuroplasticity is as real as the growth mindset. The intricate networks of the brain operate like wonderful scaffolds stacked on top of one another, so the more myelin you create, the more you stand on the shoulders of giants. Or on the shoulders of yesterday's myelin.

Up until now, all of those hard or frustrating things that have made you feel inadequate or incompetent have been things to steer clear from. Now that you can see it differently you can take the next step and invite a mindful breath before your next adventure. Struggle is no longer an enemy but a flashing neon sign that beckons you forward, further down the path of myelin and mastery. Will you do it?

REPETITION

The second ingredient of building myelin is repetition.

When I started with the national bobsled team, I was adequately strong from several years of weight training, but not bobsled strong. A new and critical lift I learned while training in bobsled was the power clean, an incredibly dynamic Olympic lift that requires power, explosion, the right timing, and great technique. I watched as seasoned bobsled veterans pulled the bar, easily catching over 300 pounds. It was incredibly frustrating for me, as even though I was squat and bench press strong, I couldn't even power clean 200 pounds. My first reaction was to think that those guys were simply naturally explosive, and that my type of strength would never be able to match theirs (notice the fixed-mindset response?).

Yet, I kept going. Day after day, week after week. The power clean became a core and frequent exercise. I practiced, failed, practiced again, succeeded—going through the natural steps of learning and development. I bet you are just waiting to hear how it turned out? Well, I'll tell you.

This guy right here, by the end of his career, could power clean almost 400 pounds.

The goal of this story isn't for you to envision how mighty and powerful I was—but you can. It's to underscore an important point. We overestimate what we can do in a day and underestimate what we can do in a year.

The more you do or see something, the more your brain adapts and layers of corresponding myelin are created. This enables you to see, notice, and respond quicker. We know this concept as practice makes perfect, but physiologically, practice makes myelin.

If you only watch professional football each Super Bowl, you aren't myelinated in noticing the method in the madness of a field full of players executing their job. You can celebrate touchdowns because points are scored and you might curse a fumble, but for the most part, the game doesn't look that different from the chaos on a youth football field. A football fan, however, who has spent hours watching games doesn't see chaos. They see precision. They've seen enough gameplay that they notice things most people don't. The same concept applies to your spreadsheets, profit and loss statement, or customer-relationship management program.

It applies to aspects of managing people, giving great feedback, obtaining strategic clarity, becoming a better speaker, negotiator, a more dynamic presenter…it's all just an exercise of quality repetition. The more you engage with something and intentionally practice through pain and discomfort, the better you'll become over time as you leverage the concept of compound interest. The more reps you engage in, the more hours you accumulate, which means more time your brain spends myelinating the things that are important.

Each time an action is repeated, myelin grows and creates faster responses and better accuracy. Which is great, unless you have created repetition that has myelinated excuses and defensiveness. The process can be a double-edged sword. The right repetition can help you on the path to mastery, but unattended and unconscious repetition can lead you into a dangerous pact with your brain, like the guy in the alley who lures you over with the sweet promises of candy only to beat you up and take your lunch money.

What you continue to do reinforces itself. The habit of taking your phone out to respond to the bells of your text messages and emails creates a Pavlovian response that caters to your reward system and myelinates the speed and accuracy of your responses. It also trims the mechanism that helps you focus your attention on other people because you are telling your brain that it isn't important. Over time, your personal relationships slowly erode as time and time again the bells and buzzes reinforce that whoever is on the other end of your telecom network is more important than the person across the table from you. This is what's happening behind the curtains of your brain. Think back to Chapter 4 and imagine the negative associations formed inside the person across from you when they experience the frequent repetition of you making your phone more important than them. They begin to myelinate a negative association about you and your inability to be present.

Some of the skills and habits you've myelinated have helped you become successful. Some of those you'll continue to use, as they are important. But it's important to understand that many of the habits you've myelinated will hold you back and prevent you from being successful as you move into more senior positions. Too many leaders still rely on the individual contributor habits that helped them in earlier roles.

ENGAGEMENT

Engagement is the third ingredient to building myelin. The more acutely focused you are during your reps, practicing intention as you exercise different skills, tools, and situations, the more resources get allocated where needed in your brain and the faster myelin is produced. How can you capture focus and engagement?

When performing keyhole surgery, laparoscopic surgeons deftly maneuver micro cameras through the body and work with tiny, precise movements.

Studies show that there is something that can help these surgeons perform measurably faster and make significantly less mistakes. All they need to do is play around six hours of video games each week. This engaged activity activates the same areas of the brain they use when performing surgery.

Engagement activates the brain and accelerates the development of myelin. Repetition alone is not enough. You can go through basic repetition and stimulate myelin, but pure, hyper-focused engagement is an activated level of awareness that seizes your full attention and harnesses your cognitive power in pursuit of precision and high performance.

Is it possible to become engaged in something that you have no interest in? Most people will say no. Let me tell you a story about a business that would never get handed down to the girl who wanted it.

When my daughter was around five years old, she once asked me to find her a game to play on Grandma's iPad when we were on vacation. The kids hadn't had much electronic exposure, but heck, we were on vacation so why not? I searched for a princess game at her request and found one called Dream Dresses. Being the nice dad that I am, I figured I'd help the sweet little girl out and learn how to play it so I could help her. So, I dove in headfirst and learned the nuances of the game. But my poor little girl never got the chance to play. It completely sucked me in.

The game was fairly complex. I was the new owner of a dress shop. At first I started small. One little sewing machine that provided a limited number of dresses for my princess customers who came into my brick and mortar store. It was your basic supply and demand concept—I'd produce the dresses they want and they'd buy them. But then different challenges started emerging. Customers would start requesting different materials and a variety of styles. My equipment couldn't produce what they requested so I had to acquire better equipment more capable of producing complex designs. I also had to consider the design of my store and where I placed certain items. I'd get customer feedback that would impact my business if I didn't respond to it quickly enough. On top of all of these business challenges, I somehow had to make time for all the dashing princes who entered the store and attempted to court me. Being the owner of my own Dream Dresses operation was a big responsibility. One that I would certainly not entrust to a small child.

I have no interest in peddling fashion to princesses. What was it that pulled me in and wouldn't let me go? I was a beneficiary (or a victim) of game mechanics.

GAME MECHANICS

Engagement is the third, vital ingredient to growing myelin. But what if you're not engaged in creating change? How can you apply a structure that, by design, pulls you in?

We play a lot of games as kids. As we get older, the games get more complex. We make rules and scream at each other if someone doesn't follow them. Sometimes we change the rules in the middle of the game and upset our friends. Creating and playing games comes naturally to us because it captures our creativity and imagination.

I was first introduced to the concept of game mechanics in Bruce Feiler's book *Secrets of Happy Families.* It was while reading this book that a huge lightbulb went off for me. Feiler broke game mechanics down into four simple elements that can capture engagement of your kids, but it also works on adults (see Dream Dresses example above).

Since the moment I was exposed to these principles in 2014, I have been weaving it into executive coaching and leadership development. It really works as a powerful structure to help focus your attention on what matters, and it also caters to activating the internal reward mechanisms in the brain. The four elements that I've adapted from Feiler's work are agency, goals, rules, and feedback. You can download your own fillable pdfs on game mechanics at www.level52.ca/leadershipacademy.

AGENCY

When I work with leaders on how to use game mechanics inside their business, I start by defining agency.

I define agency as an individual's ability to act by themselves to make plans, carry out actions, or make an informed and voluntary decision based on their knowledge and intentions. It is the ultimate position of choosing your own adventure versus being an object in someone else's adventure.

When people understand their goals, have a solid grasp of the rules they need to adhere to, when they have the feedback mechanisms in place to reinforce or course correct, then you can let them run to daylight. It's this voluntary piece that allows them to individuate and express the goal their way.

For example, if you and I have the collective goal to win the hockey game by scoring more goals than the other team, not everyone is going to contribute or do it the same way. Gretzky played hockey his way. He didn't do much around the corners but spent a lot of his time behind the net. Messier powered through people and Kurri positioned himself in space, waiting for that pass to one-time it into the net. All three were effective in their own way. How can you treat the goals and objectives in your business the same and play to people's strengths?

In the previous chapter we explored the big question, what would make this year the best year of your professional career? You need to answer this question for yourself and then work with the members of your team to answer it for themselves. This is the doorway to agency. Consider it the gateway activity that turns yourself and others into annual agents of creativity and meaning. Do it, and soon, you'll have agents running all over the place, turning their personal and team goals into reality.

Let's look at two different examples of different leaders who made game mechanics work for them.

Jane is a leader who was overwhelmed by the quantity of emails in her inbox. One opportunity that came out of her exploring the best year of her professional career was getting to inbox zero—getting to the point where there were no emails in her inbox. With a current quantity of close to 2,000, how might she achieve that?

The next example is Russell. He had been given feedback that people didn't like working with him because he always had to show up as the smartest person in the room. His objective was to achieve the opposite—he wanted to become the leader that made other people feel like the smartest person in the room.

Both of these examples offer wonderful development opportunities that would require both Jane and Russell not only to do things differently, but to behave differently. How could they navigate the treachery of new habit formation and behavior change? Once their goals were set and their internal buy-in was there, they moved to the next step: creating levels for their goals.

LEVEL UP YOUR GOALS

As a kid, I remember how frustrating it was when my parents would tell me and my brother to shut off the Nintendo and come for dinner. "But we are almost done with our level!" we would scream back, annoyed. Completing the current level and getting to the next one was the only thing that mattered in our world at that moment, and it wouldn't be stolen away from us in return for soggy cabbage rolls. Not today Pauline.

Levels are simply milestones that help you and the people you work with understand and celebrate progress. Video games have goals. You know what it takes to get to the next level— how many points or items you need to collect, whatever it is— and every level gets a little more challenging. Remember, a lack of clarity translates to inefficiency and poor productivity. Clarifying your goals and taking the time to identify levels activates an internal drive, as most people enjoy working towards the next level and celebrating progress. If they don't, it's probably a result of poor goal clarity.

Let's go back to Jane and Russell. Here we had two destinations, one much clearer than the other, but both valiant pursuits.

Jane's goal = achieve zero inbox by the end of the year.

Russell's goal = Make other people feel like the smartest in the room.

Both of these goals required new habits to be formed. In Jane's case, it was management, strategy, and prioritization of emails, whereas Russell had to first self-manage his expertise and seek to be more fascinated with others than expect they be fascinated with him.

Jane's levels were easier to measure and break down. Her goal was to have 500 fewer emails in her inbox per quarter, a reduction of over 150 emails per month, approximately 40 fewer per week, and eight fewer per day. She somehow had to find a way to continue or exceed the normal volume, while chipping away at the debt. Her first level was developing a strategy and game plan to reduce the debt of emails. From there, it was engaging in the communication and activity required to chip away.

In Russell's case it was a little more difficult to identify levels at the beginning. His goal ended up being to have not provided a single solution for people on his team if it wasn't deemed a high-risk situation. He would embrace curiosity, listen, and ask high-impact questions. He would embody the spotter. The level system he created was more of a personal, subjective analysis, but he did find a way to enroll others to help. He created his levels based on small activities that became a points system for him.

Getting to the next level can be anything from lagging results like revenue to leading activity like phone calls, presentations, prospecting, face to face meetings, or feedback conversations. The great thing is, you get to take agency and create the levels in this game of choose your own adventure.

When you find out what's important to you, create daily, weekly, and monthly levels so you can track your progress and engage the devices of your brain to help you. Your brain loves a good challenge when it knows it's within reach, so seek to level up each day or week. With hard work over the course of the year, you might even reach level 52.

FOLLOW THE RULES

In a video game, you learn the rules quite quickly. What you can and can't do. Whether you can move forward or backward. The rules clearly define what you should or shouldn't do and simply what's in bounds and out of bounds and it is reflected by points or some other measurable factor.

The same applies to your goals. Once you understand what you need to achieve to get to the next level, make rules you can follow that lead you to the activity you want.

Jane's rules for objective zero inbox:

- Create prioritization method with assistant.
- Identify emails assistant can respond to.
- Ensure emails are filed in appropriate folders.
- Set scheduled time to respond to emails.
- Respond to emails in category one (urgent + important) same day.

Having these rules in place helped Jane relax the cognitive burn that was taking place, and this enabled her to park it and pick it up in a better place with more productivity.

Russell's rules for objective making other people feel smartest:

- Read reminder before meetings (similar to a personal memo to remind him of his objective and why).
- Tell people at beginning of meetings (he told on himself at the

beginning of every meeting, so people knew he was trying to self-manage and ask questions).

- Do not give solutions, only in emergencies.
- Do not give opinions until the last five minutes of a meeting.
- Acknowledge others' thoughts and contributions before meeting is over, preferably throughout.

These rules gave Russell items to focus on when he went into each meeting. He was transparent and vulnerable with the people on his team, so they knew exactly what he was trying to myelinate.

I have seen too many brilliant people flounder in their business because so much time was spent just trying to figure out the rules of the game. What to do in certain situations, what rules activate when priorities come into conflict with one another, what the boundaries or limits are. In some cases, there may be rules associated with budgetary, resource, or time constraints. The point is, do yourself a favor and enable the people on your team to be better by marking the field you play in and developing and clarifying the rules of the game.

BACK TO THE F WORD

When you are immersed in a video game you get almost instantaneous feedback that tells you whether you are getting closer or further away from your target. It is the presence of that feedback mechanism that enables you to course correct and get back on the path of progress or create momentum by accumulating points that reinforce the right things.

What are the feedback mechanisms that will let you know if you are getting closer or further away from your goals?

In Jane's case, it was simply the reduction of emails sitting in her inbox. Her rules gave her insight into the types of emails that were coming to her different inboxes so she could develop strategies to address the different folders. In Russell's case, he developed a point system based on his rules.

Russell's rules for how he can make people feel like they are the smartest:

- Read reminder before meetings (one point).
- Tell people at beginning of meetings (one point).
- Do not give solutions, only in emergencies (two points).
- Do not give opinions until the last five minutes of a meeting (two points).
- Acknowledge others' thoughts and contributions before meeting is over, preferably throughout (three points).

Each meeting or interaction had the opportunity for Russell to earn nine points. He tracked this consistently, and each day, he sought to surpass the previous day and week's totals. It gave him something to focus his attention on, a place to evaluate the key activities and behaviors that led to a more transformative leader approach.

So, what can you develop to help you know if you are getting closer or further away from the things that are important to you? Whether it's fancy dashboards, tick marks, or dropping paper clips into a jar when you do something right, feedback systems can be simple and significant in helping you develop the habits you need to be better.

Game mechanics provide a structure that can help you focus your attention on what matters most so you don't expend significant amounts of energy trying to figure out the game you're playing and where you stand.

Try it. Apply game mechanic principles in your organization to help people celebrate progress, and create clarity through rules. If your people don't know how to level up and see the progress they are making, they will become actively disengaged. If the rules around your business aren't clear and consistent, they will become frustrated, exhausted, and disengaged. If feedback mechanisms aren't in place to reward and course correct, letting them know where they stand, they will make assumptions that might lead to undesirable results.

Get creative through the concept of game mechanics and ensure each aspect is met. It doesn't have to be an intricate process. You know those coffee cards that you want to fill up so you get that free coffee? Yup, game mechanics. It's a powerful structure that can help you focus on the right habits to deliver the results you want and engage your workforce.

BREAKING BAD AND BUILDING NEW

You understand the three ingredients of myelin growth. Struggle, repetition, and implementing structures to help you maximize engagement. Now it's just a matter of breaking those bad habits that hold you back, right? Well, here's the thing. You can't actually break bad habits. There's more to it than that.

Studies show that you can develop myelin until the day you die, but you don't *lose* myelin unless you develop a demyelinating disease. It's like that old saying, "it's just like riding a bike." You have the myelinated skills to ride a BMX bike even if you haven't ridden one in a decade. You can hop on and within a few minutes convert back into your 12-year-old, ramp-hopping self. The same applies if you learned to speak a language as a child but haven't accessed it in years. Immerse yourself in that language for a few days, and your fluency comes back very quickly because you've got the myelin.

This is great when it comes to good habits but unfortunately also means that there is no such thing as breaking a bad habit. That bad habit of being an expert who has all the answers and steals away the chance for people to think? You can't break that habit. You have to myelinate new ones.

HABITS THAT PUT YOU AT RISK

When it comes to achieving that best year of yours, you need to identify which habits to build and which to bypass. In our accelerated leader programs I ask participants to reflect on their habits and look at those habits they rely on most to be successful, for example solving problems, driving efficiency, doing the work yourself, networking, emailing, or focused work at the office.

Take a moment to think of all of the habits you've leveraged to be where you are. As you examine those habits, consider the benefits those habits have delivered. For example:

- Solving problems gets you noticed and closes gaps quickly.
- Driving efficiency makes things smoother and helps the bottom line.
- Doing the work yourself ensures the quality is where you want it and you have control.
- Networking gives you warm introductions, thought partners, and lets you collaborate with people in other areas.

Equally as important is to explore the downside of relying on these habits. Take your list of habits and now consider the potential downsides these habits might have. For example:

- Solving problems prevents other people from solving them, so you don't develop people.
- Driving efficiency might create efficiency fatigue in others.
- Doing the work yourself might get you labeled as a micromanager or someone who is a black ceiling for those wanting to further their career.
- Networking might have others feel undervalued as you constantly look outward and bypass internal relationships.

It's important for you to take inventory of the habits you rely on most and ask yourself which of these habits might be holding you back from being a better leader. Once you identify them, you can develop a game plan to myelinate new habits. Identifying them is the easy part. Committing to the process of myelinating them is a different story. It will take struggle and repetition.

What would you do if you couldn't rely on these habits to be successful? You'd have to get creative.

CREATIVE CONSTRAINTS

If you've ever had someone in your life experience a stroke and survive, you will know that they experience weakness and paralysis to one side of their body. The rehabilitation is often long and challenging, and it's incredibly frustrating to not be able to perform some simple tasks like getting dressed, eating, and taking a shower.

The worst thing someone can do in this situation is learning to compensate for their deficiencies with the non-injured side. Doing so significantly decreases the chances that survivors will regain function on their injured side because they just simply use the side that works.

Some of the best and fastest rehabilitation occurs by using a process called CIMT. CIMT stands for Constraint-induced Movement Therapy, which restricts usage of the uninjured side for up to 90% of the waking day. Restricting the healthy side forces survivors to put their effort and energy into rewiring the brain and regaining their independence. This is an example of a creative constraint.

Creative constraint is an innovation theory that suggests that well-designed constraints improve creativity. Removing certain things from your environment forces you to examine life without them. This practice is used by design thinkers and innovation experts, and it can help you greatly as you seek to myelinate new habits that make you a better leader.

At Level 52, our programs introduce the examples of strokes and creative constraints to help leaders develop creative ways to bypass the habits they rely on most, or those they want to bypass and focus more acutely on what they want to develop. For example, one leader I coached tended to give long, verbose answers and stories to every question I asked and wanted to develop the skill of brevity. I challenged him to pause and answer every question with only one sentence. If he didn't, I would make annoying buzzing sounds like he'd just lost in *The Price is Right*.

Another example of a creative constraint is one that can help prevent the person with the loudest voice and the biggest opinion from driving the result during group collaborations. After a question is posed, take two minutes of silence during which everyone writes down their answers on a sticky note and posts it on the board.

What do you rely on most to be successful? Take it away for a day, or even a week. Test your adaptation capability. Using creative constraints will help accelerate developing new habits and skills that will help you succeed as a leader and make the best year of your professional career a reality.

You'll either do it, or something wild and weird might show up randomly that forces you to learn and work differently. Let's get really creative and imagine what that might be. How about something unimaginable, like a pandemic?

CONCLUSION

You now know that developing new skills is all about developing new myelin, and that struggle, repetition, and engagement will help you get there. To get engaged or create engagement in your teams, you can implement the principles of game mechanics in your leadership. Experiment with creating levels for goals, identify rules, and explore feedback mechanisms. Most importantly, you need to make the goals meaningful.

'Breaking bad habits' is hard because you're actually developing new ones, and those habits you've relied on to be successful can also put you at risk. By identifying the downside of your habits you can engineer ways to bypass them, by, for example, introducing creative constraints.

Myelin is the last element in the Science Behind Success™ metaphor. In the next chapter, I will pull it all together and you will begin building your individual leader playbook to help you deliver meaningful leadership inside your organization.

THINGS TO REMEMBER

- Myelin is the insulating sheath that surrounds nerve fibers and increases the speed of impulses. It is the physiological representation of skill.
- The ingredients to developing myelin are struggle, repetition, and engagement.
- Create engagement by using Game mechanics: clear goals, rules, feedback and agency.
- Creative constraints remove what you rely on most so you can innovate and myelinate new skills and habits.

CREATE MEANING

Awareness: Where am I having a hard time getting traction on my own or my teams' goals?

Intention: Where can we intentionally incorporate elements of game mechanics to help create our best year?

Exercise: Break down a single goal into levels, create clear rules, and identify creative feedback mechanisms.

Reflection: Set a calendar reminder to evaluate your progress and make the necessary shifts to enhance your progress. Remember, everything is an experiment. Get better information to make better adjustments.

7

YOUR LEADER PLAYBOOK

Now that you've activated a positive deviant and meaningful masochistic mindset, you see the pains in your world differently. You've exercised them and spread intentional viruses as you deliver your authentic brand into the environment. You unapologetically take a stand for what's important, and you have embraced transformational leadership to help people create the best year of their professional career. You've exercised the inputs that create powerful expressions and meaningful relationships, and you've implemented creative constraints to bypass bad habits and develop good ones.

What's next? All this content is absolutely useless in itself unless you do something about it. And doing something once won't lead you to that powerful legacy you envisioned. So how do you get good at being that leader you want to be? What does it take to be your best when it matters most? That's right, practice.

In this final chapter, I am going to give you the final missing pieces that will enable you to leverage and practice high performance principles to deliver meaningful leadership.

WHAT ARE YOU SKILLED AT?

What is something you are skilled at? Do you play an instrument? Are you a carpenter? Can you work with electronics? What helped you build this skill? Have you taken the same approach when it comes to your leadership?

When was the last time you practiced your leadership? I mean, really practiced your leadership. I often ask my clients this, and they go, "What do you mean, practice my leadership? I'm leading all the time." No you aren't.

Remember, practicing means pushing your boundaries, situational learning, and exercising the muscles required to deliver what you intend to deliver. It's about building an awareness around how to respond in a situation. It's developing skill and awareness through repetition.

If you're like most leaders, you don't practice your leadership in this way. Most leaders lose the intentionality required to really lead powerful teams. They step into their role and lead the particles, or details of the business, and not the people. They assume a new position and do what they've always done, because that's what they've practiced. It's what they know.

This is where you need to change for yourself and the people you work with. It's time to step into extreme intentionality and utilize a high performance method. It's time to shed the expectation that you are a perfect leader, that fixed mindset will eventually screw you if it hasn't already. I have seen too many leaders beat themselves up over a situation that they didn't respond well to. Tough luck. Pain is a biological requirement for growth so you can either learn or fail. Use those micro-pains that go along with exercising your leadership so you can accelerate your impact through intentional practice.

Our equation that leads to daily acceleration is:

W/U + EX + C/D = ML.

Warm up + exercise + cool down = meaningful leadership.

IT'S TIME TO WARM UP (W/U)

Leadership and all of the elements that fall into the bucket of leadership are simply muscles that need to be exercised. The more that you exercise them intentionally, the more you're going to increase your fitness and decrease the likelihood of significant injury when you trip over a hurdle. Because it will happen. The more you reach and push, the more you're going to trip. So how do you increase your fitness, your ability to recover quickly and keep moving forward?

Next, I'm going to introduce you to a high performance practice that's used by the world's best athletes to accelerate results. I use this method when I work with leaders, and, when done consistently, it always creates significant results. It starts with identifying what your warm-up is. Don't make the mistake of running into your day without a proper warm-up. High performance athletes warm up for over an hour before they engage in challenging training exercises, and meaningful leaders warm up before engaging in their daily leadership challenges. Far too many leaders just jump into their day, increasing the likelihood of injury. Do it right and start your day with a solid foundation. Consider your warm-up a brief investment of time that increases the likelihood of you having a better, more consistent impact.

The objective of the warm-up is to enhance your leadership fitness by exercising extreme intentionality and a consistent leader brand. We do this by asking some personalized questions to help leaders review their leader brand, goals, and intentions. Below is a sample question set with common questions leaders we work with use. Review these questions to stimulate thought on what your warm-up questions might be and choose the ones that feel best. There is a worksheet you can use while you do this at www.level52.ca/leadershipacademy.

1. Who are the people in my life I am grateful for?

2. What recent opportunities am I grateful for?
3. What is my brand promise?
4. How will I specifically express this today? How will I know?
5. If I only did one thing today to create my best year, what should it be? Why is it important?
6. What skill do I need to exercise today? Where and when will I do it?
7. What is the authentic brand I am delivering into my world today? How will I do it?
8. What challenging situations do I need to meet head-on today?
    a. What do I want the outcome to be?
    b. What's the impact I want to have?
    c. What do I know about myself that will help me do this well?
9. What perspective do I want to reframe before I start my day?
10. What viruses do I need to spread today?
11. What viruses do I need to stop?
12. Today is an exercise—how hard will I push myself towards excellence?
    a. What risks need to be taken to avoid easy street?
    b. What micro-pain needs to be addressed before it becomes acute? How will I do it?
13. What do I want to create today?
14. What powerful intentions need to be set?
15. Who do I need to thank or recognize today?

16. What do I need to remind myself of (values, mantras, intentions, guiding principles)?

Once you've got your questions, it's up to you to start exercising what's most important. There are many ways you can structure your warm-up. Here are a few examples:

- Book time in your calendar that links to a Google Form that records your answers.
- Have your EA call you at a specific time each day to interview you.
- Write in a journal.
- Capture your answers in a program like One Note, Evernote or a Google Doc.
- Record a voice memo and play it on your commute to work.

WHY WARM UP?

You're probably a cheater. If given the chance and knowing you wouldn't get caught, you'd probably cheat. In 'The Dishonesty of Honest People: A Theory of Self-Concept Maintenance,' Nina Mazar, On Amir, and Dan Ariely[25] looked into the conditions that would have good, honest people cheat.

In their studies, they engaged students in a problem-solving task made up of 20 puzzles. Each participant was instructed to solve as many puzzles as possible within four minutes and told that two participants chosen at random would be given $10 for each correctly solved puzzle, making it possible to earn a total of $200 if they got all of them right. To a student, $200 is a significant amount of money.

At the beginning of the experiment, participants in the first group were

25 Mazar, Nina, Amir, O., and Ariely, D. (2008). 'The Dishonesty of People: A Theory of Self-Concept Maintenance.' *Journal of Marketing Research,* 45(6):633-644. [Online]. Available: https://journals.sagepub.com/doi/10.1509/jmkr.45.6.633

primed by having to recall 10 books they had read. The second group were asked to recall the Ten Commandments. As we learned in Chapter 5, priming is an effective tool to point your focus in a specific direction. How did it influence the participants in this study?

Many of those in the first group ended up recording an incorrect score in an attempt to maximize their own gain. But no one in the second group did.

Replicated studies with non-religious affiliations yielded similar results. Moral benchmarks provided by codes or values have a significant impact in raising desirable behaviors, like honesty.

Moral reminders can eliminate cheating and in the context of leadership, can eliminate behaviors that are incongruent with your brand. We are all human and can be pulled to the dark side in situations of stress, depletion, or when certain conditions are in place. This is important knowledge that leaders can use to their own personal advantage from a character and legacy standpoint.

That's why you build your warm-up. So you don't end up doing something stupid. I forgive you if you blasted past the warm-up section before this and thought it was stupid. Go back and read it again. Then start building your warm-up. To help you, use the pdf at www.level52.ca/leadershipacademy.

YOUR DAILY EXERCISE (EX)

As a meaningful leader, every action in your day is an opportunity to exercise something. When you fully embrace your brand and the pursuit of greater awareness, you identify the exercises that matter most. It's very easy to go through the motions and rely on the muscle memory of your leadership, and at times you'll need to, but don't miss the opportunity to sculpt and shape the leadership muscles you want to develop.

When kept up to date, your CSP inventory (complaints, stressors and pains) will provide an important lens to help you determine which exercises matter most to you and create the impact you want to have. By using this resource and seeing your days as an opportunity to exercise those important leadership muscles, you'll soon develop a ritual, much like brushing your teeth. Removing the plaque that can build up over time will prevent decay and degradation of your leadership effectiveness that could result in a painful extraction or root (cause) canal.

COOL DOWN (C/D)

Most people would agree that experience is their greatest teacher, yet we generally do a terrible job of leveraging our experience daily to accelerate our wisdom and capabilities. Just like a good warm-up is important, your exercise isn't complete without something at the back end.

Athletes cool down after their exercise and assess the state of the union. What worked well? What didn't? A meaningful leader reflects on the impact of their leadership so they can accelerate their awareness and also their impact. They create time at the end of the day for this critical cool down. A cool down allows you to challenge your assumptions, analyze your performance, and reflect on what's most important. This will, over time, enhance your cognitive agility, ensure consistency in your leadership, and allow you to deliver a consistent and intentional impact in your environment. Building in time for reflection expands your awareness and strengthens the muscle of challenging your assumptions, enhancing your leadership fitness and accelerating your wisdom.

I challenge leaders that work with me to create moments in each day devoted to the development of their leadership. These moments include their warm-up at the beginning of the day, their cool down at the end of the day, and maybe also some reflection or planning in-between. Ask yourself, what is my practice? What is my warm-up, and what is my cool down?

Below is a sample question set with some of the most common questions leaders we work with use to cool down. Review these questions to stimulate thought on what your cool down questions might be and choose the four or five that feel best.

1. What is my purpose/mission/brand promise? How did I exercise this today?
2. Who are the people in my life I am grateful for?
3. What am I proud of?
4. What recent opportunities am I grateful for?
5. What was most challenging today? What can I celebrate? What will I do different next time?
6. What perspective am I stuck in? What assumptions do I have that I need to be cautious about?
7. What obstacles showed up today that frustrated me?
    a. What do I need to exercise as a result?
    b. Why is this important?
8. What frustrations arose today that I need to take responsibility for?
9. What am I stressed out about that I need to let go of?
10. What am I taking control of that I need to delegate?
11. What will I do differently tomorrow?
12. What am I most proud of in how I showed up today?
13. Based on what happened today, what change is wanting to happen?
14. What needs to be different tomorrow? How do I need to show up differently to make sure it happens?
15. What acute pain will I address tomorrow before it becomes chronic? How will I do it?
16. What will I make most important tomorrow?
17. Who will I thank or recognize today?

Now that you've got your cool down questions, you can start experimenting. You can use the same variety of methods to structure and record your cool down as you did for the warm-up, for example voice notes or Google Forms.

A PLAYBOOK OR A BLUEPRINT?

Everything you've done up until now has prepared you for this moment. You've got the mindset, you are clear about your leader brand, and you have a shiny new transformational tool kit that is spilling over in abundance. It doesn't stop there. On top all of this, you've designed the best year of your professional career and have used game mechanics to develop the new habits that will get you there. Lastly, you've just put thought and effort into building your warm-up and cool down, elevating you into the upper echelon of meaningful leaders. If not now, then soon.

The last step in your journey is to build out your playbook. I use the term playbook because it's different from a blueprint. A blueprint tells you the way. It's the 'truth' based on rules and calculations and is intended to be replicated exactly. A playbook, however, is a documented hypothesis. An organic tool that is meant to orient you to the fundamentals of your leadership in challenging situations. Just like a playbook in football guides you when the other side of the ball comes out in certain formations, the playbook you are about to put together is a simple one-page guide that will help prepare you for the things that matter. You can download it at www.level52.ca/leadershipacademy.

YOUR LEADERSHIP PLAYBOOK

CURRENT VERSION OF YOUR BRAND PROMISE

Write down the current version of your brand promise. Revisit it every quarter to ensure it still reflects the authentic, aspirational, and unapologetic elements of who you are and what you want to bring to your environment. Beside it is a space for you to add an image. Call it a logo, a symbol, whatever it is, add something that goes beyond words and has meaning to you. This will ground the meaning of your brand promise and help make it a part of you.

MY LEADER PLAYBOOK

Brand Promise:

Brand Image:

NEW HABITS

Remember that exercise where you explored making this the best year of your professional career? You'll need some new habits to help bring that to reality. Write down the three habits that you'll put a strong focus on (using game mechanics) and myelinate the hell out of them.

OLD HABITS

Out with the old and in with the new. It's ok to grieve letting go of old habits, but you have to empty the closet to get some fresh new clothes. Here's your chance to finally bypass those old habits that no longer serve you. Make it hard to use these habits and identify some creative constraints to help you

3 new habits that will help me be successful:	3 old habits that will hold me back:
1. ____________	1. ____________
2. ____________	2. ____________
3. ____________	3. ____________

WE'VE GOT A SITUATION

Studies show that leaders who envision how they deal with challenging situations well in advance, tend to operate with more consistency and confidence when under fire.

At the bottom of your one-page leader playbook you are going to identify some situations that either threaten to, or have already brought out a negative brand representation in you.

As you identify these situations, think about how you may have responded in the past that was damaging to your relationships and your brand. Now imagine the greatest expression of you when you are on-brand. How would you have navigated the situation or how do you envision dealing with it intentionally and unapologetically?

Record these situations and the intentional response you see yourself having.

Situation:	**Intentional Response:**

CONCLUSION

In this chapter, I introduced you to the final piece of the puzzle to mastering your leadership and the Science Behind Success™: Practice. Consistent, intentional practice.

It all starts with a good warm-up to prime you for your leadership practice every day. Then, of course, it comes down to exercising the challenges and opportunities that show up every day. Sometimes you'll deliver your best performance, and there will be times you don't. The cool down is just as important, providing you with an opportunity to reflect, adapt, and accelerate your growth. Our one-page leadership playbook forms the backbone of your leadership practice. Use this to record and keep track of your brand promise, your habits, challenging situations, and how the best version of your leader brand should handle them.

Keep your playbook handy, reference it frequently, and make adjustments when you get new information. It's part of the meaningful leadership practice and it goes back to fully immersing yourself in the Science Behind Success™ method—the pursuit of greater information and using that information to grow.

THINGS TO REMEMBER

- Start each day with extreme intentionality by setting yourself up for success. A consistent warm-up will increase the likelihood you are on-brand and avoid injury.
- Every day is an opportunity for you to exercise those leadership muscles that will make you meaningful. Identify these situations and what it is you're exercising.
- Accelerate wisdom by carving specific time each day to reflect and build awareness around your intended and unintended impact.
- Identify the situations in your past, or ones you foresee that might take you off-brand. Envision how you might best deal with these situations and exercise them.
- Keep your playbook visible and adapt it as new information gives you a new level of awareness to shape your intention.

CREATE MEANING

Awareness: What scenarios in this upcoming year do I want to show up as the best version of my leader brand?

Intention: How will I intentionally warm up to deliver the best version of my leader brand?

Exercise: Build out your leader playbook and use this as an ongoing tool to remind you of the habits to focus on and the scenarios to prepare for.

Reflection: Set a reminder in your calendar to revisit your playbook. It's an organic document that will become more valuable as you engage in your daily exercises and leverage your learning.

CONCLUSION

I hope you made this the book you came to read. Whether you are in the C-suite and are rebranding or myelinating new habits or just entering the workforce and developing the right habits from day one, thank you for taking on meaningful leadership.

Changing the way you engage with the stressors in your environment and activating meaningful masochism will differentiate you in a good way. When you combine this powerful mindset with the extreme intentionality of an authentic and unapologetic brand, your executive presence and followership will undoubtedly enable you to create great things. When you hold fervently to your role as a culture custodian and actively choose the viruses you remove or allow inside your organization, you'll generate an irresistible space and a profound expression of yourself and those you work with. By activating the 'spotters' approach and the inputs that affect expression, your legacy will be significant and you will accelerate the growth and capabilities of your team. By harnessing the power of meaning as you drive to create the best year for yourself and those you work with, you can provide the structure and support to make it real. All of this is achieved through the little things that make a big difference.

What happens after you put down this book is more important than the insights you had while reading it. The forgetting curve and powerful vortex are real forces that will steal this time back and keep you from creating the impact you want. Whether it's getting into a Level 52 program to continue exercising it, working with one of our coaches to personalize it, or creating a group that you can collaborate and hold accountability with, do it. Knowledge is only potential power, so it's up to you to convert it into something meaningful.

I left you with a cliffhanger at the beginning of Chapter 6. Remember Doug, that crusty CFO turned COO who was on the back nine of his career? Instead of clubs, he carried the nasty scythe of the grim reaper and had gotten feedback that invited him to change his style. How did he do? Did he take the path of least resistance and bulldog his way through the next year and carve up the course, or did he embrace the challenge, become intentional about his brand, create the conditions for success, and myelinate a new transformational tool kit?

Over the course of a year, Doug rolled up his sleeves. Instead of coming into our sessions wearing a grimace, his eyes started to soften and he carried a smile. He committed to getting out of the way, empowering his people by truly stepping back and spotting them so they could take on bigger challenges and drive the operations of the organization. When I solicited his peers for feedback, many of them chuckled at how disorienting it had been for them at the beginning to see Doug catch himself in meetings and struggle through applying the tools, but because he was transparent about it, they wanted him to succeed. They became champions for him in his transformation and became an essential part of his feedback mechanism.

Doug underwent a significant transformation from an entirely transactional leader to one who had experimented and witnessed the benefits of a transformational focus. There were definitely moments where he frustratingly called bullshit, but he recovered and stayed the course.

When our year-long engagement ended, we reviewed the last piece of feedback and created a revised playbook for him to take forward. Before I left his office for the last time, I said, "Hey, Doug. You asked me a question at the beginning of our relationship. You asked me if I could teach an old dog new tricks. What's the answer to that?"

He paused and sat back, putting his hands behind his head. He smiled and said, "It depends how much that old dog wants to learn."

Doug is one of my favorite stories. At Level 52, we work with leaders in several different stages at several different levels, but Doug's was truly a story of transformation. I brought the method, and he brought the hunger, humility, and meaningful masochism to make it happen.

Everything out there in the leadership space that promises to develop you to be a better leader is nothing more than a method. Whether it's this method or another method, nothing works unless you work it. To work it the right way, you need to make it meaningful.

So back to the big question that keeps you up at night. How will you myelinate hypertrophic memes within your leader epigenome? You choose.

ABOUT LEVEL 52

Level 52 is a boutique leadership and executive coaching firm that works with leaders around the world. For over a decade, Jayson and the Level 52 team have worked with leaders and organizations from Singapore to Silicon Valley. Level 52 has provided its core services of executive coaching, leadership programs, or keynotes to leaders in organizations like: Baker Hughes, Ikea International, IBM, Toyota, Jabil Circuits, Facebook, Ripple, Google, LinkedIn, professional sports organizations, Olympic athletes, and many others. We continue to be told the same thing, "Our work is different."

What makes it different? It's a little bit of the content and the unique structure of the programs, but for the most part it's more about our relentless focus on how the content is applied to make a difference to that leader's world. To create the intentionality, structure, and rigour to exercise the right things, in the right way, to become a meaningful leader making a meaningful impact.

The name Level 52 is inspired by structure and progression. There's a saying that you overestimate what you can do in a day and underestimate what you can do in a year. So at Level 52, we seek to help leaders create a structure and process to up-level the areas that are important to them over a 52 week period. The focus on structure, and little shifts, become big gains over the course of the year. That's simply how to accelerate transformation.

www.level52.ca

RECOMMENDED READING

The following books have in some way, big or small, influenced and inspired certain elements of this book. I recommend you read some, or all of them. I have inserted them into where I think they fit best in relation to our four pillars of hypertrophy, memetics, epigenetics, and myelin.

HYPERTROPHY

Dweck, Carol S. *Mindset. The New Psychology of Success.*

Duckworth, Angela. *Grit.*

Holiday, Ryan. *Ego is the Enemy.*

Holiday, Ryan. *The Obstacle is the Way.*

Heath, Dan. *Upstream.*

Frankl, Viktor. *Man's Search for Meaning.*

Siegel, J. Daniel. *Mindsight.*

Weisinger, Hendire and Pawliw-Fry, J.P. *Performing Under Pressure.*

Willink, Jocko and Babin, Leif. *Extreme Ownership.*

Kotler, Steven. *The Rise of Superman.*

Sinek, Simon. *Start with Why.*

Sinek, Simon. *Leaders Eat Last.*

Hollis, James. *What Matters Most.*

Brach, Tara. *Radical Acceptance.*

Mullainathan, Sendhil and Shafir, Eldar. *Scarcity: Why having too little means so much.*

MEMETICS

Dawkins, Richard. *The Selfish Gene.*

Kahneman, Daniel. *Thinking Fast and Slow.*

Brodie, Richard. *Virus of the Mind: The New Science of the Meme.*

Gladwell, Malcolm. *The Tipping Point: How Little Things Can Make A Big Difference.*

Gladwell, Malcolm. *Blink: The Power of Thinking without Thinking.*

Ariely, Dan. *Predictably Irrational.*

Berger, Jonah. *Invisible Influence.*

Berger, Jonah. *Contagious.*

Cialdini, Robert B. *Influence.*

Goldsmith, Marshall. *Triggers: Creating Behavior That Lasts—Becoming the Person You Want to Be.*

Buckingham, Marcus. *First, Break all the Rules: What the World's Greatest Managers Do Differently.*

Thaler, Richard. *Misbehaving.*

Pink, Daniel. *To Sell is Human.*

Gutsche, Jeremy. *Better and Faster.*

EPIGENETICS

Lipton Bruce H. *The Biology of Belief.*

Lipton, Bruce H. *Wisdom of Your Cells.*

McTaggart, Lynne. *The intention Experiment.*

Christensen, Clayton M. *The Innovators Dilemma.*

Maltz, Maxwell. *Psycho-Cybernetics.*

Pink, Daniel. *When: The Scientific Secrets of Timing.*

Collins, Jim. *Good to Great.*

Christensen, Clayton M. *How Will You Measure Your Life. Harper Business.*

Whitworth, Laura, Kimsey-House, Karen, Kimsey-House, Henry, Sandahl, Phil. *Co-Active Coaching.*

Markova, Dawna and McArthur, Angie. *Collaborative Intelligence.*

Blumberg, Matt. *Startup CEO.*

Drucker, Peter F. *Effective Executive.*

Lencioni, Patrick. *The Advantage.*

Novak, David. *Taking People With You.*

Hubbard, L. Ron. *Dianetics.*

Grant, PhD. Adam. *Give and Take.*

Coyle, Daniel. *Culture Code.*

Catmul, Ed and Wallace, Amy. *Creativity Inc.*

Knapp, Jake. *Sprint.*

Cashman, Kevin. *Leadership from the inside out.*

Dispenza, Joe. *Becoming Supernatural: How common people are doing the uncommon.*

Marcus, Aubrey. *Own the Day, Own Your Life.*

Asprey, Dave. *Super Human.*

STUDIES:

Weaver, Ian C.G, Cervoni, Nadia, Champagne, Frances A., D'Alessio, Ana C., Sharma, Shakti, Seckl, Jonathan R., Dymov, Sergiy, Szyf, Moshe, and Meaney, Michael J. (2004). 'Epigenetic programming by maternal behavior.' *PubMed* 7(8):847-54. [Online] Available: https://pubmed.ncbi.nlm.nih.gov/15220929/.

EurekAlert! 26 July 2010. 'Plentiful maternal affection in early infancy boosts adult coping skills.' [Online] Available: https://www.eurekalert.org/pub_releases/2010-07/bmj-pma072310.php

Champagne, Frances A. and Curley, James P. (2008). 'Epigenetic mechanisms mediating the long-term effects of maternal care on development.' *Neuroscience and Biobehavioral Reviews*, 18 January 2008.

PBS Nova., 'Epigenetic Therapy.' Interview with Dr. Jean-Pierre Issa at the M.D. Anderson Cancer Center. [Online] Available: https://www.pbs.org/wgbh/nova/genes/issa.html.

MYELIN

Coyle, Daniel. *The Talent Code.*

Gladwell, Malcolm. *Outliers.*

Duhigg, Charles. *Smarter Better, Faster.*

Duhigg, Charles. *Power of Habit.*

Clear, James. *Atomic Habits.*

Doidge, Norman. *The Brain that changes itself.*

Epstein, David. *Range.*

Feiler, Bruce. *Secrets of Happy Families.*

Schwartz, Barry. *Paradox of Choice.*

Keller, Gary. *One Thing.*

Foer, Joshua. *Moonwalking with Einstein.*

Doerr, John. *Measure What Matters.*

Heath, Chip and Heath, Dan. *Switch.*

ACKNOWLEDGMENTS

"Spring has passed. Summer has gone. Winter is here… and the song I meant to sing remains unsung. For I have spent my days stringing and unstringing my instrument."

— Rabindranath Tagore

For several years, I'd say "this is the year the book gets done." Each year would pass, and it would still be incomplete. I can finally stop saying that.

It has been with the help of several important people that this book has finally come to fruition. Aside from the pandemic that slowed the pace of our business so I could create space to get it over the finish line, I have been so fortunate in my career to have a long list of champions that have provided insight and feedback as this idea went from a concept, into constant iterations, until finally the book you are holding.

Every great idea starts with a catalyst, and if it wasn't for my relationship with Steve Mesler, this book would never have been conceived. Steve has always been a collaborator, inspiration, and champion for this book and the work we do at Level 52. Level 52 and this book would likely not have existed if it weren't for the support and tenacity provided by my dear friend and teammate, Shelley McKenzie.

There have been leaders in my life who have had a significant impact on the way I lead and who inspire me and drive my aspirations. Mikell Rigg-Parsch, Lee Maclean, Jill Schicter, Brian Tucker, and Paul Byrne have been constant benchmarks and models of meaningful leadership, each in their own way. To the friends and colleagues who have supported me and listened to me year after year: Ben Clarke, Pablo Molina, Nathan Ciccoria, Alec and Gavin Harrison and many others. To the team at Happful, Calvin Simpson and Susan Gaigher, for helping create the structure to bring this book across the finish line and providing the expertise in editing, design, and publishing. Thank you.

And of course, to my family: Mom, Dad, Tamara, Darren, and my wife Kelsey, for their undying support, unconditional understanding, and for being there to provide feedback and a helping hand, always.

Thank you to the amazing contractors, consultants, and team members who have contributed to the work we do at Level 52 to create meaningful leaders. And finally, thank you to my clients, past and present, many of whom who have become close friends. Thank you for being willing lab rats and for allowing me and the team at Level 52 to become your trusted advisors. Thank you for continuing to drive a higher bar for meaningful leadership inside your organizations.

Manufactured by Amazon.ca
Bolton, ON